NURSULTAN
NAZARBAYEV

A Life Story of the
first President of Kazakhstan

NURSULTAN
NAZARBAYEV

*A Life Story of the
first President of Kazakhstan*

S T A C E Y
INTERNATIONAL

NAZARBAYEV
A LIFE STORY

Stacey International
128 Kensington Church Street
London W8 4BH
Telephone: +44 (0)20 7221 7166
Fax: +44 (0)20 7792 9288
Email: info@stacey-international.co.uk
www.stacey-international.co.uk

First published (Russian edition): Astana, 2012

Hardback edition ISBN: 978-1-909022-29-4
Paperback edition ISBN: 978-1-909022-39-3

Design: Christina Forde
Editorial Coordination: Philippa Neville
Translators (from the Russian): Ronan Loughney
                                 Jeremy Stopes
                                 Ivo Graham
                                 Katyuli Lloyd
Production: Elizabeth Holmes
Project Management: Hannah Young

CIP Data: a catalogue record for this title
is available from the British Library.

Printed and bound in Turkey.

Acknowledgements
This book is produced with the financial support of the
Foundation of the First President of the Republic of
Kazakhstan – the Leader of the Nation.

Preceding pages:
A panoramic view of today's Astana, the capital
city of Kazakhstan, conceived and ordained by
Nursultan Nazarbayev.

Contents

PROJECT DIRECTOR

M.B. Kassimbekov, Ph.D in Political Science, Professor

This book is the translation of the following work into English:
Nursultan Nazarbayev, Biografia (*Nursultan Nazarbayev, Biography*)
Astana: Delovoy Mir, 2012, 304 pages.

Introduction

Any history of the evolution of the independent Republic of Kazakhstan is unequivocally linked with the name of its founder and first President – Nursultan Abishuly Nazarbayev.

This book is the first attempt at an official historico-biographical study of the life and governance of N.A. Nazarbayev. It follows his life's journey from a simple rural childhood to national leader.

Most detailed attention is devoted to his political biography, given as a historical reprise of the dramatic and unpredictable events and outcomes that shaped the evolution of Kazakhstan, on the lip of the twentieth and twenty-first centuries.

A broad range of archive material contributes to this work. This biography is the most dependable documentary source to date on the recent history of Kazakhstan. This, as well as rich photographic and illustrative material, makes the book specially valuable; but most valuable of all are the facsimile copies of personal documents which allow the reader to become immersed in the atmosphere of the events being described. This work is thus aimed at a wide range of readers.

1

The Home Border

In the 1940s Chemolgan was a typical Soviet village, with thirteen streets, divided by the river, no asphalt roads and no street lighting. Cars and tractors were a rarity and people usually traversed the fields by foot, river or horse. In the summer a bridleway came into use, for shepherds leading their flocks from the valley to higher mountain pastures. Of the better-class older houses that had survived the Soviet government's confiscation from the kulaks, there were only ten, the rest merely temporary buildings. There was a space between each dwelling of some 150–200 metres. In the centre of the village was a nucleus of Party buildings, the village council, four state farms, a bakery and a school (D.A. Furmanov, K.E. Voroshilov, May 1st and Enbekshi).

Abish's family.
In the front row from left to right – Bolat (son), Anipa (daughter).
In the second row – Nursultan (son), Alzhan (wife), Abish.
In the third row – Satybaldy (son), Zeynegul (nephew).

Chemolgan was characterized by its mixed population: as well as Kazakhs, it included Kyrgyzs, Tatars, Uzbeks, Uighurs, Dungans and, from the turn of the twentieth century, Russians, Ukrainians and Mordovians. From the 1930s political exiles started to be settled in Kazakhstan, and, over time, many other nationalities of the USSR would migrate to there.

Nursultan's father – Abish Nazarbayev (1898–1971) – was from Koshek branch of Shapyrashty tribe of the Senior Horde. He was the son of the district head and judge, Nazarbay Sapakbayuly, who died in 1901. Following the early loss of his father at the age of eleven, Abish was hired out as a farm labourer to the Nikiforovs, a well-to-do Russian family, where he acquired both a certain hardihood and his first professional skills. Thanks to his industriousness and thirst for knowledge, in contrast to his peers, Abish learnt Russian as well as how to plough, run mills and master shoemaking. He even owned a small horticultural and trade businesses, which was a fairly rare occurrence given his background. Given the limitations of education at the time, Abish was not able to complete his schooling. Like that of many people of his generation, his school environment was primitive and harsh.

Being the head of the family, Abish worked in a variety of jobs when he was young. From 1927–30, he took part in one of the most important projects of the first five year plans of the USSR – the construction of Turksib, the railway network, which links Central Asia and Siberia. From the middle of the 1930s he took a lead role in the creation of the Ushkonyr state farm and after its liquidation in 1939 he joined the D.A. Furmanov collective farm, originally taking charge there of the field team which looked after crops. In 1940, whilst saving cattle and farm property from a fire in one of the winter mountain huts, he suffered burns and injured his arm. Despite his disability he continued to head the field team on the farm.

Nursultan's mother – Alzhan Nazarbayev (1904–77) – was born in the mountain village of Kasyk (now known as Talapty) in the Kordai region of Zhambyl, into the Zhatkanbay family, mullahs of Kaskar origin. She was a clanswoman of Dulat of the Senior Horde. Later, her ties to this religious family led to persecution at the hands of the Soviet authorities. Despite this hardship, Alzhan always kept her cheerful disposition, clearly evidenced in her propensity for practical jokes and spontaneous bursts of song. Throughout her life she was both a happy housewife and employee at the collective farm.

Above:
Abish Nazarbayev.

Below:
Alzhan Nazarbayev.

Opposite top:
Satybaldy Nazarbayev.

Opposite middle:
Anipa Nazarbayev.

Opposite bottom:
Bolat Nazarbayev.

Nursultan's parents met on the Turksib building site, where Abish was appointed as chief of recruitment and Alzhan's family, along with many other immigrants, were rounded up for compulsory work.

Abish and Alzhan married in 1934. The first six years of their marriage were spent childless and so they greeted the birth of a long awaited heir with boundless joy, seeing it as a reward for their love, belief and patience.

According to the customs of their ancestors, the honorary right to name the newborn child fell to the eldest in the family, Grandma Tetebala, who was essentially head of the family after the death of Granddad Nazarbay. Along with Nursultan's parents, she played a big role in her grandson's upbringing.

The infant was baptized by the name Nursultan, which is a combination of the name 'Nur' – from the Arabic for light, radiance, cleanliness. In the Koran 'An-Nur' is one of the ninety-nine names of Allah, and 'Sultan' is from the Arabic for elite ruler, sovereign, aristocrat or lord. Amongst family, friends and contemporaries, the name Nursultan was used in its simple and casual form 'Sultan'.

The widespread custom where grandparents symbolically adopted their grandsons gave boys the hierarchical status of their father's younger brother, meaning that, in interfamily relations, Sultan called his grandmother 'Appa' (mother), his father Abish 'Aga' (elder brother) and his birth mother Alzhan 'Zheneshe' (wife of eldest brother).

After Nursultan, his parents had three futher children: his brother Satybaldy (born 1947), his sister Anipa (born 1950) and his brother Bolat (born 1953).

Until the age of five Nursultan never left Ushkonyr, where, as the head of the cattle-breeding brigade, his father herded the state-farm flock. A beautiful place, Ushkonyr is situated at the foothills of the Ili Alatau mountains and considered one of the country's most glorious regions.

All of Nursultan Nazarbayev's ancestors had lived in this area, working in peaceful, creative occupations as cattle-herders and tillers of the earth, or defending the land from hostile intruders with weapons in their hands.

One of his eighth-generation ancestors was a famous infantryman, Karasai Batyr Altynayulı (1589–1671), who actively participated in the Kazakh war liberation from their Jungar conquerors. Ever since, as a sign of respect for Karasai's military prowess, his name has served as a war cry for his Shapyrashty kinsmen.

'All for the front, all for victory.' Posters from the time of the 'Great Patriotic War' of 1941 to 45, in which the Soviet people ultimately overwhelmed the formidable invader, Nazi Germany.

Nursultan's grandfather Nazarbay is also firmly stored in people's memories. He was an active supporter of the transition to a sedentary, non-migratory lifestyle and did a lot to ease the transition of tribesmen into agriculture. Ever since, in these places there remain the names 'Nazarbay Mill' and 'Nazarbay Field', derived from the work he did.

In Ushkonyr there were three long cabins, in each of which lived ten families, all employed in the management of 5000–6000 cattle. In the same place was the sub-Moscow biomedical factory branch, where workers converted animal blood into serum.

It was here the Nazarbayev family faced 'The Great Patriotic War' of 1941–45. The war, affecting every area, did not bypass Abish's home. In view of his disability, by which he was deemed unfit for military service, he began ensuring – together with others in a similar situation – that the army base had food provisions and agricultural materials. As well as feeding his own family, Abish and Alzhan took it upon themselves to help the families of their relatives, friends and neighbours, whose breadwinners had been called up to army service. The work places of those at the front were filled by women, old men and children, who were obliged to work 12–14 hours a day.

As was the custom of the time in such a social scene, the young Nursultan got his training in sheer hard work, helping his parents, and as he grew older took on an ever bigger role: he cared for the family herd and domestic birds, carried water in buckets, split firewood, shovelled coal and looked after the garden, bringing cleanliness and order to the home. On entering adulthood, he would characterize these years by their deprivation of 'the black bread of childhood' (a symbol of beauty and

goodness in life), an impression which melded into his conscience as if on 'one single winter's night, hungry and cold'. Yet even as children he and his kin were ingrained with the deep belief in the correctness of their country's actions, which would result in the countrywide mobilization of their continued spiritual and physical strength.

In the final year of the war, Nursultan reached the age of five, but already he strongly felt affinity with the fate of his homeland. After half a century, he would recall how 'the first word we heard in our childhood was "Fatherland", warming our cold hands by the oven in our peasant huts and baking bread for all. A thousand kilometres from our mountain village blazed the fire of the Great Patriotic War. From the front arrived

Above:
Chemolgan Middle School, named after D.A. Furmanov.

Below:
Kaskelen Kazakh Middle School, named after Abay (c.1950).

13

"the black papers", letters of condolence for the old members of the village, for close and distant relations and even for the young of neighbouring homes who had still not even completed school. The heart-rending cries of mothers. The terror of children. The grief of the parents, having lost their only son ... of children justly compared to guiltless angels, whose mouths spoke their most cherished beliefs. Staring at our grief in the oven's hearth, we found our role in the war, struggled with the enemy and, repeating what we had heard from our elders, prayed for our homeland.

'At the end of it all, our pleas were heard, we were victorious. Then, standing by the oven ranges of our farmhouses, as in the memorable month of December 1986 and other critical moments in our life's story, that glowing hearth and a vivid sense of my homeland melded into my consciousness like a palpable object, each indivisible from the other. On the sky-blue flag of Kazakhstan, with so much history behind its achievement of independence, is depicted the sun – the universal flame. This isn't only a reflection of the strength of nature and the cosmos – it is the flame in the hearts of our forefathers and of those yet to be born, representing the realization of their dreams.'

The war took the lives of a hundred thousand peasants, and across all the countries of the Soviet Union, more than 20 million people. Of those who survived and returned home from the battlefields, tens of

Above:
'We, the champs.' The young Nursultan, one from left.

Below:
Nursultan's first teacher, T.A. Ismailova.

14

thousands died from injuries and illnesses, whilst many were undeservedly imprisoned. Yet, despite this, the former soldiers actively joined in with the post-war rebuilding of the country.

All these sights and experiences established a sense of deep gratitude to the older generation in Nursultan's mind, for their sacrifice and victory, and the fact that they had ensured a peaceful existence for their successors. From this point he would persistently direct his strength to surrounding such ex-servicemen with respect, care and security.

From these years stem the definitively antimilitary, pacifist focus of his worldview, emphatically condemning war and its destructive effects, disrupting and disfiguring society and often leading to the loss among people of a humane outlook on life in general.

Broadly, the deep change in the experience of the family of Nursultan Nazarbayev was to reflect, as in a drop of water, the dramatic events that fell on the Kazakh nation in the twentieth century.

Subservience to imperial sovereignty, World War One, the emancipatory rebellion of the Kazakhs in 1916, Russia's February and October revolutions of 1917, the rise and fall of the Alash Orda regime,

Tenth-grade class register from Abay Kaskelen Kazakh Middle School, graduating class of 1958.

the bloody fratricidal civil war of 1918–20, the founding of the Soviet authority and the formation of the Soviet Kazakh Republic, Goloshchokin's 'Little October' and the consequences of forcible collectivization and transformation of the Kazakhs to a non-migratory mode of life, resulting in the terrible famine of the 1930s and the mass exodus of the Kazakhs from the confines of the USSR, the Science Power Plant and its deactivation, mass political repression by a totalitarian regime, the deportation of political prisoners to Kazakhstan, the widespread construction of gulags in Kazakhstan, the suppression of the political, ethnocultural and linguistic rights of peoples in their own land to a degree never before endured in history, all played their part in Nursultan Nazarbayev's emergence into the public arena.

Then and thus had Kazakhstan become a republic of the Soviet Federation, formed in 1922 under the name 'the Union of Socialist Soviet Republics' – the USSR.

Kazakhstan's evolution during the Soviet period had multiple consequences for the Kazakhs. On one side was an attainment of formal

Abay Kaskelen Kazakh Middle School leaving photograph (Nazarbayev, second row, fifth from right).

autonomy with the foundation of a distinct administrative territorial border, large-scale industrialization, the end of illiteracy, the guarantee of public access to free education and medical services, and national construction projects. On the other side ensued huge losses to their ethnographic integrity, a real threat of losing their mother tongue and forgetting their traditions and historical roots, as well as the catastrophic degradation of their ecological surroundings.

In 1948 Nursultan Nazarbayev entered first grade of the Kazakh-Russian middle school named after D.A. Furmanov (since 1999 known as Karasai Batyr School) in the village of Chemolgan, where his first teacher was T.A. Ismailova, teaching him from first to fourth grade.

In the first two grades, young Nursultan lived in his uncle Umbet's house, since his parents' own home was not in Chemolgan at the time. After this period his parents got a house there and finally settled in Chemolgan. With characteristic foresight, Abish bought a home on Podgorni 'beneath the mountains' Street, in the upper part of the village where well-off Russians lived, so that through them Nursultan could master their language.

From this time, his mother engendered an atmosphere around Nursultan encouraging the acquisition of knowledge, strict discipline and the fulfilment of his growing responsibilities. In the hours that Nursultan studied at home, quiet would set in, and the boy's school friends were not usually allowed over to the house before he had finished his homework. After playing with his friends, hungry for knowledge he would often sit by a kerosene lamp into the early hours, seen by his parents as an heroic feat. Only Nusultan was allowed to light a lamp outside of 'study' hours. His parents, due to the hard times in which they grew up, had been unable to get so much as a basic education. They struggled to ensure their son got all that he could out of his small village school.

Not all the local children were able to attend school; some of them, on the very edge of poverty, simply did not have the clothes or shoes. In Kazakh language classes, the number of students only reached between eight and ten. But there was a benefit to this; each pupil received more personal attention from the teacher. During a single day of study the children were tested on five or six subjects, which called for a high degree of diligence in preparing for their homework.

At the Chemolgan school Nursultan's teachers were M. Ikhamberdin and K. Omarov in Kazakh language and literature, T. Sultanbekov in Russian language and literature, S. Mukanov in History, P. Esimova in

Mathematics, Z. Karasayev in Physics, M. Shapenov in biology and N. Shlykov in physical education and 'military-patriotic' education.

According to his teachers and peers, learning came easily to Nursultan, and he never had to expend much energy on it. He was very attentive and possessed a perspicacious mind and a good memory, retaining everything he learnt over the years, and hence was bound to be a good student. However, Nursultan himself realized quite early on that one's natural talents cannot alone lead to deep, firmly established knowledge. Each and every discipline called not so much for mechanical processes of learning as for a form of study that penetrated to the heart of the matter at hand.

Quite early on, a natural inclination towards creativity manifested itself in Nursultan. Under the influence of his grandmother, even at the age of five Nursultan was able to quote a fairly broad range of excerpts from folk tales. Afterwards, as with many of his peers, he was captivated by adventure stories, but the modest village library was not able to meet all he sought. The lad got to read absolutely everything he could lay his hands on. A passion for reading would serve him well in the future, broadening his knowledge and, in time, giving him the ability swiftly and productively to work through large and thematically complex swathes of information.

By the age of twelve, Nursultan was performing on the stringed dombra and harmonica to a decent standard, composing Russian and Kazakh songs on them, giving pleasure to his listeners. To pay for his own harmonica, he worked through the summer for his neighbour making him tea and the like. Later, having noticed the pull music had on his son, his father ordered a handmade dombra from a local craftsman, which Nursultan mastered under the tutelage of his relative A. Kolzhasaruli. At the same time, Nursultan started to write his own verses and songs, at first derivative and naive, but over the years increasingly original, mature and thoughtful.

Despite relative proximity to the capital, life in Chemolgan suffered the lack of a cultural life like that of the big cities. Long holidays were limited to film-showings, cultural parades and the occasional visits of distinguished literary and artistic figures.

Physical education and sport had a meaningful place in Nursultan's life. For the boy, having grown up in traditional rural surroundings, these were the national Kazakh sports: Kazaksha Kures (a type of wrestling), Kokpar (contesting on horseback for a goat carcase), Baige (games revolving around racing), Audaryspak (a kind of horseback sumo

A snapshot of lifelong friends taken on the last day of school (Nazarbayev crouching, centre).

wrestling), Tartyspak (a team game on horseback), Asyk (loosely similiar to marbles) and the like. Though of gentle disposition, Nursultan delighted in encouraging competition amongst his peers, himself becoming an ardent trainer and strict referee.

Lacking sports equipment, the young boys set up their own chin-up bar, barbell and exercise board and sometimes weighted their legs with boulders or logs. In the winter, students went sledging and built snow towns and, in the summer, bathed in the streams of the clear, rapid mountain river. In the chess club, run by the teacher T. Sultanbekov, the children readily mastered the ins and outs of checkers, chess and the Kazakh national game Togyz-kumalak.

However, most of the time Nursultan, like most of his peers in the village, spent his time on more serious matters , helping his parents with their demanding farm work.

In the summer months his father was always on the cornfields, and his mother on the beetroot acres. Hence, Nursultan took up a separate farming role, one which the Soviet power termed the new 'serf'. There

19

On the threshold of adult life.

was little machinery to hand. Farm labouring consisted of extremely taxing physical tasks which paid not so much a living wage as what might be called 'subsistence pay'. It was subject to strict territorial and social restriction on farmers without passports, a lack of access to many everyday materials and social benefits and services and crassness and opportunism by those in authority regarding welfare of the town and countryside – all tactics which sowed the first seeds of doubt in the justice of the system of state control in the USSR.

With the aim of lessening the crop shortfall, the government allowed farmers to sell surplus goods at market prices as 'subsidiary agricultural products'. But the little money which Abish and Alzhan gained from selling the crops and vegetables cultivated on the farm plot was not even close to meeting the family's needs. In 1948 a change in the rationing card system gave the Soviet people some relief and breathed life back into a measure of market economy. However, records show that in these years under the rule of N.S. Khrushchev, opportunism pitched the country from crisis to crisis. The unsustainable stimulation of agricultural production, the sudden hikes in tax and the confiscation of farms triggered a new wave of desolation and a lack of hope for what tomorrow would bring. One bitter episode would burn into Nursultan's mind forever, when, in answer to the introduction of absurd taxes on horticulture in the countryside, his father angrily and sadly ploughed up his favourite garden which he had made with his own hands.

Being the eldest child in the family, attempting to help his parents to swiftly alleviate their poverty and raise his younger brothers and sisters, after graduating from seventh grade Nursultan decided to quit school and go to work. But having listened to all of his son's arguments, the distressed Abish convinced him to release himself from the demands of work and continue his studies. And just in time. Not long before this, in recognition of his punctuality and active social work, Nursultan Nazarbayev had been taken into the first ranks of the Komsomol, the Young Communist League.

In 1957, due to a lack of students, the tenth grade of Chemolgan School was closed, and in order to continue his education, Nursultan and six classmates were forced to transfer to Abay Kaskelen Middle School, situated in the centre of the region – the village of Kaskelen.

The school's students welcomed the new students from Chemolgan, providing them with shelter, food and clothing. However, wanting to ensure the best living and study conditions for Nursultan, and attempting to shield him from the potential influence of wayward classmates, Abish refused the offer of state support. Despite his limited means, he rented a flat for his son.

Teachers and senior members of the village were quick to fall in love with the young arrival from Chemolgan, as he became for them not only the best student and pride of the school but a keen volunteer in his extracurricular and social work, which students took up upon entering the school, and then through his work as secretary of the Komsomol.

The independent thought, intellectual bravery, sharpness of wit and inquisitiveness with which this boy from Chemolgan posed questions to teachers, often plunged not only the young but also senior pedagogues into confusion. Nazarbayev's favourite history teacher, S. Isayev, being both vice-head and Party organizer, remembered that during these years 'The History of the Kazakh SSR' was not taught as a separate discipline but was included on the curriculum of 'The History of the USSR', where just three hours were dedicated to the history of Kazakhstan. One day in class Nursultan posed a question: 'When teaching us the history of the USSR, you speak from the very beginning and in detail about the evolution of the state of Russia, its economic and cultural development, as well as its kings, founders and national heroes. Why then, concerning

ЮННАТЫ. 1951 г.

The 'young naturalists' group. Nazarbayev in the back row.

the history of Kazakhstan, Kazakh rulers and war heroes, are we forced to gather information not within the walls of the school and not from textbooks, but, in any meaningful form, from family stories, from conversations of the elderly sitting on the walls outside our homes?'

To meet the eyes of the whole class and challenge such a curriculum, in which attention was not allocated specifically to the national republic, could well have been a professional and, more seriously still, an inexcusable political mistake. The teacher held the student back after class and in a long, open conversation, backed him. 'When they allow us more hours, we will study the history of Kazakhstan in as much detail as possible. In the meantime, come and see me outside classes and I will try to answer whatever questions you wish.'

During staff meetings, teachers often pointed out that when studying new material, Nazarbayev loved to make interdisciplinary links and attested to the soundness of his knowledge, along with his desire to construct a comprehensive, logically consistent and multifaceted worldview.

His teachers were responsible for shaping this talented, disciplined and serious youth, focused beyond his years, and who had a vivid sense of duty and fairness across the gamut of his life, according to A. Bayzhanov (Headmaster), S. Isayev (Deputy Head, History), Z. Abdullina (Russian language and literature), A. Askarov (Biology), G. Beysenbetov (Kazakh Language and Literature), U. Igelmanov and B. Kenzhekeev (Mathematics), Z. Ertaykyzy, R. Kattalov, K. Konkashbayev, R. Sarbasova, A. Sarybayeva and various others. Nursultan held precious memories of all these teachers as well as well as of his classmates, many of whom went on to become distinguished specialists – servicemen, economists, accountants, teachers, metallurgists, civil servants, freight transporters, and engineers.

Active civil involvement, a broad outlook and an irreproachable moral reputation made Nursultan an indisputable leader, evidence of which emerged in his personal bearing. In holiday parades on the festive days of 7 November and 1 May, he was given the honour of being the school standard bearer and marching at the front of the procession.

One revealing example occurred in the years of political rapprochement between the USSR and China and the strengthening of the Soviet-Chinese friendship when as a demonstration of trust he was accorded the right to correspond with a young teacher from No. 5 Middle School in the town of Qigong in China's Sichaun Zhou Xiao Bai Province. Dated 5 November 1957, a letter from a Chinese citizen was initially received by the All-Union Leninist Young Communist League's Central Committee, after which it was sent to V. Kurdin, secretary of Kaskelen district committee of Komsomol, to whom it arrived in February 1958. On the instruction of the editor of the regional newspaper *For Communism*, U. Tastanbekov, and his editorial colleague, they found their Chinese comrade a pen friend, proposing the tenth-grade student Nursultan Nazarbayev. The two letters were published on the pages of the thirtieth edition of the regional newspaper, released 16 March 1958. Later China and the USSR's relationship worsened due to a breakdown in communication and armed border conflicts. This reason alone separated the pen friends.

Approaching graduation from comprehensive school, the school year group spoke out solidly in favour of presenting Nursultan with the gold medal (denoting the highest academic achievement). However, by reason of pedantry and a narrow-minded, bureaucratic regional educational authority, and a superfluous comma in his final composition, the school changed its examination mark for his composition from 5 for 'excellent' to 4 for 'good'. The result was the all-rounder Nazarbayev being awarded the silver medal. School Director A. Bayzhanov and teacher of Russian language and literature Y. Bayer acted on behalf of the student and contacted the Minister of Education. But the administration was adamant and would not entertain reconsidering what had already been decided. Only rather different circumstances allowed for this: to be awarded the gold medal it seemed one needed to be the offspring of a leading government official. However, Nursultan did not become despondent, because before him lay the enticing and unexplored horizons of a single-minded adult life.

Scientifically inclined education and political propaganda of this period popularized awareness of those in romantic professions such as airline pilots, geologists, captains of ocean-going vessels, engineers, builders, performers of experiments, those who achieved startling records or who made famous discoveries or performed acts of valour. Nursultan had dreamed of undertaking comparable ventures of such pioneering and high-profile male professions, which above all gave such people high social status and good jobs.

Full of honourable thoughts and belief in his own capacity, Nursultan was sent to Alma-Ata, where he applied to the chemistry faculty of the S.M. Kirov Kazakh State University. He passed the entrance exams, but in the end misfortune awaited him; it turned out that, for entry to the faculty, he fell short by one mark.

Nursultan was not able to return to the village and reconcile himself to defeat. Concern for his reputation was not the issue. His personal priorities were clear enough. First of all, he had to honour the expectations of his parents, teachers and neighbours, and next, he needed to vindicate his yen for education. His potential for self-realization in the village had been exhausted. Having hit a barrier he must make his way in life and attain the status of a notable citizen. From that point he focused his existence on this fundamental, ever-present objective.

He became a temporary security guard in a bank, working there for three months. But the aggressive demeanour of such people compared to his own kind, and the hurt he felt to his pride, encouraged the young man to think intently and search for a role more worthy application of his ability.

Hence, in that summer of 1958, in Alma-Ata he sat an entrance exam for the Kiev Institute for Civil Aviation. Passing the competitive selection process at the Kazakh Soviet Socialist Republic Administration

Opposite:
A page from the Kazakh newspaper *Kytaidan Khat* (16 March 1958) compares letters exchanged between Nazarbayev and a Chinese pen-friend, Zhou Xiao Bai, in support of Chinese-Soviet friendship.

Қытайдан хат

Қытай халық республикасы Сычуань провинциясы, Цзыгун қаласындағы 5-ші орта мектептің жас оқытушысы Чжоу Бай-Сяо ВЛКСМ Орталық Комитетіне хат жазып, советтік бір жас азаматпен таныстыруды өтінген. Бұл хат және оның суреті Қаскелеңдегі Абай атындағы орта мектептің оқушысы Нұрсұлтан Назарбаевқа тапсырылды.

Төменде Чжоу Бай-Сяо жолдастың хаты мен суретін және Абай атындағы қазақ орта мектебінің оқушысы, жас комсомолец Назарбаевтың достық жауабын беріп отырмыз.

Совет Одағы Бүкілодақтық Лениншіл Коммунист Жастар Одағының Орталық Комитетіндегі барлық жолдастарға!

Сәлеметсіздер ме.

Ұлы Октябрь социалистік революциясына 40 жыл толды. Совет халқы Коммунистік партияның даңышпан басшылығының арқасында өткен 40 жылдың ішінде адамзаттың айқын болашағы үшін, бүкіл дүние жүзіндегі бейбітшілік үшін күресе отырып, саясатта, экономикада және мәдениет саласына бұрын көрмеген жеңістерге жетті. Дүние жүзінде бірінші болып жердің жасанды серігін ұшырды. Жер шарындағы бейбітшілік жақтайтын барлық адамдар Совет Одағының ғылым саласындағы осы зор табысына сүйсіне қарап отыр.

Ұлы Совет халқы және Коммунистік партияны Ұлы Октябрь социалистік революциясының 40 жылдық мерекесімен шын жүректен құттықтаймын!

Мен мектеп табалдырығын жаңа ғана аттап, халық мұғалімі деген абыройлы қызметке орналасқан комсомолецпін. Мен ерте кезден бастап-ақ Совет Одағымен жете танысуға құмар едім. Ол үшін Совет Одағымен бір комсомолецпен байланыс жасауды ойлайтынмын. Бірақ ол арманым осы күнге дейін орындалмай келеді. Сол себепті ВЛКСМ Орталық Комитетіндегі жолдастардан мені советтік бір жас досыммен таныстыруды шын жүрегім өтінемін. Ол маған неғұрлым көбірек хат жазып,

дос жүрегімен танысып тұрса екен.

Мен осы хатыммен бірге өзімнің тауда түскен суретімді және Янцзы өзеніне салынған көпірдің суретін жіберемін. Мұны менің досыма табыс етулеріңізді сұраймын.

Біздің тіліміз әдет-ғұрпымыз әртүрлі болса да шын достық сезімі бізді біріктіріп отыр. Бұл достықты ешқандай күш бұза алмайды.

Маған хатты мына әдреске жазуға болады: Қытай халық Республикасы, Сычуань провинциясы, Цзыгун қаласы, 5-ші орта мектеп Чжоу Бай-сяо. Қытай мен Совет халықтарының мызғымас достығы жасасын! Сіздердің денсаулықтарыңызға тілектеспін. Қытайдықтың,

ЧЖОУ БАЙ-СЯО,
5 ноябрь 1957 жыл.

Суретте: Янцзы өзенінің көпірі

Алыстағы қытайлық досыма

Сәлеметсіз бе.

Совет Одағының ВЛКСМ Орталық Комитеті Сіздің өтінішіңізді орындап, Сізбен хат жазысып, достық байланыс жасап тұру үшін Сіздің хатыңызды маған жіберіпті. Сонымен қатар, мен сіздің хатыңызды, суретіңізді және Янцзы өзеніне салынған көпірдің суретін алдым.

Сізбен хат жазысып, достық қарым-қатынаста болуға шын жүректен қуанышты бірімін жайдә түсіп, сіздің арманыңыз — Совет Одағымен жете танысу болса, Сізге қолымнан келгенінше көмектесуге дайар екенімді білдіремін.

Алдымен, Сіздің хатыңызға жауапты мүша көшіруге себепкер мен емес екенімді айтып, кешірім сұраймын.

Мен Қазақ Советтік Социалистік Республикасының Алматы облысы Қаскелең ауданы Қаскелең селосының Абай атындағы орта мектебінің X-класында оқимын. Бірінші класты бастап, бүгінге дейін өте жақсы оқып келемін. 1956 жылдан бері комсомол қатарындамын. Менің әке-шешем осы Қаскелең ауданының Ворошилов атындағы колхозының мүшелері.

Социализм орнату жолында орасан зор табыстарға жетіп отырған Ұлы Қытай халқының комсомолымен тығыз байланысы жасап танысу біздің әрқайсымыз үшін зор қуаныш. Ал осы мүмкіншілік үлесіме тиіп отырған мен шексіз қуанышты екенімді тағы да қайталап айтамын.

Біздің советтік Отанымыздың жастары, сүйікті Коммунистік партияның зор қамқорлығын ескере отырып, әруақытта өз Отанына пайда келтіруге тырысады. Ал мен орта мектепті бітірген соң жоғары оқу орындарының біріне түсіп, келешекте коммунизмнің саналы құрылысшыларының бірі болсам деп ойлаймын.

Менің Сізге өте көп сұрақтар қойғым келеді, бірақ бір хатқа оның бәрін сыйдыру мүмкін емес және бұл хатым тек таныстық хат. Келесі хаттарда бір бірімізден көп нәрселерді сұрап білуге толық мүмкіншілігіміз болар деп сенемін. Бұл хатымды осымен аяқтаймын.

Сіздің құрметті оқытушылық қызметіңізде тамаша табыстарға жетуіңізге шын жүректен тілектеспін.

Асыға хат күтемін. Советтік досыңыз

Назарбаев Нұрсұлтан.

Менің адресім: СССР, Қазақ Советтік социалистік республикасы, Алматы облысы, Қаскелең ауданы, Қаскелең селосы, Абай атындағы қазақ орта мектебі. Назарбаев Нұрсұлтан.

16 ноябрь 1957 жыл.

САЙЛАУШЫЛАР ҮШІН

Шамалған станциясы. Станцияның клубында сайлаушылар жиналысы болды. Оқытушы Қ. Райымханов жолдас «Дүние жүзіндегі ең демократиялық конституция» деген лекция оқыды.

Бұдан соң сайлаушыларға «ВЛКСМ-ның 30 жылдығы» мектебінің көркемөнерпаздары үлкен концерт қойып берді. ВЛКСМ-ның 30 жылдығы атындағы мектептің бірто

оқушылары мен мұғалімдері Жиынғылды разъезіндегі темір жолшыларға концерт қойуға жүріп кетті.

М. ҚОЙШЫҒҰЛОВ.

Астық тиегішке тұқым дәрілейтін тетік орнатылды

ОРАЛ. Өткен жылғы көктемде Краснов совхозында жүгерінің барлық тұқымы — 80 мың центнерге жуық тұқым механикалық әдіспен дәріленетін болатын. Мұның үшін арнаулы түрде жабдықталған „ЗП-40" астық тиегіш пайдаланылды. Астық тиегіштің өзегіне жаңғыша шағын ғана бункер орнатылды. Тұқым автомашинаға тиелген кезде бункердегі улы дәрілер аз-аздан тұқымға араластырылып құйылып тұрады. Содан кейін бұл дәрі астық тиегіштегі тұқымға тегіс тарайды. Осының нәтижесінде тұқымды тиеу және оны бірдей дәрілеу арқылы совхоз 15 мың сом үнемдеді. (ҚазТАГ).

Қазақстанның тың жеріне қоныстанушылардың жаңа тобы келді

Ақмола және Қарағанды облыстарының тың жерді ауданда тауда түскен колхоздары мен совхоздарына январь мен февраль айларында Белоруссия ССР-нен 200 семья көшіп келді. Жаңадан қоныстанушылар ауыл шаруашылығының тәжірибелі қызметкерлері.

Тың жердегілер жаңадан қоныстанушыларды қуанышпен қарсы алды. Бұл жерлердегі ертерек жылдарда келіп орналасқан оларды жерлестері мен тұысқандары қоныстанушылардың келуіне қатты қуанды. Жергілікті шаруашылықтар жаңадан келгендерге несие беріп, азық-түлікпен көмек көрсетуде. Мемлекет оларға үй салып, енар сатып алу үшін ұзақ мерзімді несие беруде.

Жеміс, жидек, жүзім өндіру артты

ЖАМБЫЛ. Өткен жылы көктемде облыста төрт жеміс-жүзім совхозы құрылды. Жаңа шаруашылықтар 184 гектар бау және жүзімдік екті. Көзір бұлардың жемін ұлғайту жұмысы жүргізілуде. Жаңа шаруашылықтар отырғызылатын шыбықтарды өздері өсіре бастады.

Болашаққа арналған жоспарда 1965 жылы жүзімдіктің бауын және жидектің көлемін 6 мың гектарға дейін жеткізу белгіленген. Жүзімдіктер толық жемін бере бастаған кезде 25 мың тоннаға дейін жеміс беретін болады. (ҚазТАГ).

Қазақстанның жүн өнеркәсібі

Жамбылда жүнді алғаш рет өндейтін фабрика құрылысында бас корпустың ірғесін қалау басталды. Бұл кәсіпорын 1961 жылы өнім бере бастайды.

Қазір республикада дайындалатын жүннің 70 проценті жуылмаған күйінде Россия Федерациясына және Украинаға жөнелтіледі.

Семейдегі фабриканың кәзіргі өзінде-ақ қайта құрылуы және Жамбылдағы жаңа фабрика жүнді өндеу мөлшерін республикада едәуір арттыруға мүмкіндік береді.

Жүн өндіретін аудандарда жүнді өндеуді қамтамасыз ету үшін Қазақ ССР халық шаруашылығын өркендетудің жеті жылдық жоспарында Қостапайда, Оралда арнаулы жаңа фабрикалар салу көзделген.

Жүн мата өндірісі ұлғайтылады. (ҚазТАГ).

Суретте: экскурсияншылар өздігінен жүретін астық тазартқыш комбайнды көреп тұр.

Оралда селолық шеберлер жасаған машиналардың көрмесі ашылды. Бұл көрмеде Оралдың № 8 механикаландыру училищесінің өндірістік оқу мастері Леонтий Михайлович Горбонтың конструкциясы бойынша жасалған, өздігінен жүретін астық тазартқыш комбайн көрсетілді. Машина астықты өзі алып, өзі тазартады және автомашинаға өзі тиейді.

Суретті түсірген В. Деликов (ҚазТАГ-тың фотохроникасы).

Редактор У. ТАСТАНБЕКОВ.

Редакцияның адресі: Қазақ ССР, Алматы облысы, Қаскелең ауданы, Қаскелең селосы, Пушкин көшесі, № 8 үй. Телефондар: редактор 1—86, секретарь 2—36
Алматы облыстық баспа басқармасының аудандық баспаханасы. Зак. № 140

of Civil Aviation and gaining entrance to aviation school, Nursultan returned to his home village with this happy prospect.

Yet unexpectedly, at the family enclave, to which the elder tribes people were also invited, his initiative was not approved of. Those attending were against his departure to a foreign land. Brought up to respect the elder generation, and not inclined to disagree with his elders and wanting not to anger his parents, Nursultan obediently accepted their verdict and after a trip to the capital, collected his documents.

The cruel twists of fortune, and the wild ups and downs which befell Nursultan that single summer, brought him deep spiritual hurt and his first serious awakening. His desire to advance into adulthood honourably, uphold the stability he had grown up with, to gain good employment and, through self-motivation, to become a fully fledged member of society, was ineradicable.

Alma-Ata (photo taken in the 1950s).

The first iron and steel works in Kazakhstan, and the forerunner of the Karaganda Metallurgical Factory, was the Kazakh Metallurgical Factory built in Temirtau in 1944 on the advice of the USSR State Committee of Defence. On 7 February 1943 it decreed 'the construction and founding of an iron and steel company' as an enterprise producing profiled iron and metal sheets. The factory duly fulfilled its brief both during the war and post-war. But it was not able to satisfy the growth of demand in the country for metal. A new and more powerful factory was necessary – for the supply of metal to the industries of Kazakhstan, to the Soviet central, Asia as a whole and to businesses of the European regions of the USSR.

Thus geographically strategic, politico-economic and ideological reasons provided the raison-d'être for the installation of a new industrial giant in the centre of Kazakhstan.

Temirtau was seen at the time as a moderately large source of labour among the gigantic construction sites near the manmade lake named Samarkand in the surrounding steppe. No industrial complex existed at that time, but an electrical centre and a first blast furnace were included in the construction project.

Together with other workforce recruits, Nursultan visited the dormitories situated beyond the River Nura in the village of Tokarevka, 14 kilometres from Temirtau. There he lived for two months. At this point the Soviet-Kazakh government took the decision to send a group of home-grown youngsters for recognition at the Soviet Union's 'Source of Manpower' – D.E. Dzerzhinsky Metallurgical Factory in Dnieper, Ukraine. There the No. 8 Main Technical Academy competently managed labour resources on behalf of the USSR Council of Ministers. Thus, in November 1958 Nazarbayev, along with a number of compatriots, was sent to study in Dnieper in the Ukrainian Soviet Socialist Republic.

At college Nursultan, being physically strong and psychologically robust, stood out among the group. There they learned how to be blast furnace attendants. Actively involving himself in education, he started to master comprehensively specialized disciplines, studying building and the principles of blast furnace operation, technical smelting and casting, as well as how to work with technical equipment and machinery. He was blessed with an understanding of theory, picking up professional competencies and skills in daily industrial tasks on the plant. During this period, despite an extremely rigid and strict daily routine whereby students were at work eight to ten hours a day, Nursultan did not forget the lessons learnt from sport, attending combat classes with the trainer L.R. Ezhevsky. The young man did not miss a single lesson, training till drenched in sweat, becoming the regional interdepartmental competitor. After a year, he achieved 'first rank' status.

The establishing in central Kazakhstan of such a giant entity as the Karaganda Metallurgical Factory, and later as the Karaganda Metallurgical Plant, was due to the area's uniquely favourable provision of all the basic components for metalworks. The vicinity had rich deposits of charcoal, steel and manganese ore, limestone and dolomites, including the local iron ore deposits at Atasuskoe, Sokolovs-Sarbaiskoe, Lisakovsk and Kachar, and Karaganda's opencast coal. Their proximity and the reliability of supply of the Karaganda region offered the prospect of long-term exploitation. The basic goods were all in reach. The idea of building a factory in Kazakhstan with full metallurgical capabilities emerged in the 1930s, attributable to the vision of the academic K.I. Satpayev.

2

Trial by Fire

In March 1956 the Central Committee of the Communist Party of the Soviet Union and the Council of Ministers of the USSR decided upon the construction of the Karaganda Metallurgical Plant. In April 1958 the Komsomol Central Committee announced at its eighth Congress that Kazakh Magnitka was a key Komsomol building, and called upon young people to support the project. Thousands of young men and women responded to the call, not just from all corners of the Soviet Union but from other socialist countries such as Bulgaria, Poland, Czechoslovakia, and the German Democratic Republic.

Having read about the project in the newspaper *Leninist Change*, Nursultan Nazarbayev decided that he too would make the journey. This time his father did not attempt to talk him out of it. After obtaining his travel ticket from the Komsomol District Committee, by September 1958 he had arrived at Temirtau.

In the volcanic heat of the blast furnace.

Nursultan's choice goes to show the way in which successive Nazarbayev generations unwittingly followed in one another's footsteps. Just as his parents had taken part in the construction of the Turksib (Turkestan-Siberian Railway), here was their son, meeting the demands of the age, present at the origins of Kazakhstan's first metallurgical institute.

The birth in central Kazakhstan of a giant like the Karaganda Metallurgical Plant, which would later become the Karaganda Metallurgical Kombinat, was due mainly to the area having a favourable combination of all the basic components of the metallurgical cycle in rich reserves of coal, iron and manganese ore, limestone and dolomite (in the the Atasusk, Sokolovsko-Sarbaisk, Lisakovsk, and Kacharsk iron ore reserves and the Karaganda coal basin). These reserves were close by and sufficient for exploitation on a long-term scale. Karaganda was well sited for transport links with the main consumers. The idea of building the plant in Kazakhstan for these metallurgical purposes dates back to the 1930s and stemmed from the academic K.I. Satpayev.

The dawn of metallurgy in Kazakhstan, and the predecessor of the plant in Karaganda, was the Kazakh Metallurgical Plant, built in Temirtau in 1944 in accordance with the State Defence Committee's decree of 7 February 1943 'On the Construction and Restoration of the Steel Industry', as an enterprise to produce high quality sheet and rolled iron. The plant fulfilled the duties given to it in the war and postwar years. But it could not meet the region's growing metal needs. A new and much more powerful plant was needed – one that could supply metal to industry in Kazakhstan, other Central Asian republics, and the businesses of the European portion of the USSR.

These were the factors prompting the creation of a new industrial giant in the centre of Kazakhstan.

Temirtau at that time was a small village in the middle of a huge construction site near the manmade lake of Samarkand, surrounded by feather-grass steppe. The plant didn't yet exist, though the electric power plant and the first blast furnace were under construction.

Together with the other recruits Nazarbayev was billeted in a workers' hostel in the village of Tokarevka, on the other side of the river and 14 kilometers from Temirtau. There he lived for two months. By that point the government of Soviet Kazakhstan had taken the decision to send a group of indigenous young men to the recognized Soviet Union training ground, the Dnieper Metallurgical Works named after Felix Dzerzhinsky, in Ukraine, where successful work had been done by

Above:
Sworn comrades, Nazarbayev (right) with Ukrainian trainee Nikolay Litoshko.

Below:
Nazarbayev's certificate of merit, November 1959, received from Dniprodzerzhynsk School, north Ukraine.

Right:
Tired but happy – on reaching
the weekend.

Below:
Blood brothers: Nursultan
Nazarbayev and Nikolay Litoshko.

the Eighth Technical School of the Main Administration of Labour
Reserves under the Soviet Council of Ministers. So it was that in
November 1958 Nazarbayev was part of the group of young Kazakhs
sent to study at Dniprodzerzhynsk, in Soviet Ukraine.

In the school Nazarbayev, being a physically robust and psychologically
mature young man, was placed in a group to be taught the profession
of furnace-tending. He took an active involvement in his studies, and
began to develop general and specialized disciplines, studying the design
and function of the blast furnace, smelting and moulding technology,
and how to work with the equipment and heavy machinery. As well as
a grasp of the theory, the students obtained professional skills as part of
their daily course of practical training at the plant. The strict and
demanding schedule kept the students busy for eight to ten hours each
day. But Nazarbayev did not neglect his sporting pursuits, visiting his
trainer L.R. Ezhevsky for wrestling sessions. The young man did not
miss a single class and would train until he dropped, winning
competitions at city, regional and inter-departmental level. After a year
he had reached first-class standard.

Success was not long in coming. On 4 November 1959,
Nazarbayev's excellent training and active participation in both the
social and Komsomol sides of school life saw him awarded a certificate
of merit by the Dniprodzerzhynsk city's Ukrainian Komsomol branch.

Despite the warmth and friendliness which they met in the Ukraine,
a stay in a foreign country far from their usual environment was a daily
struggle for the young Kazakhs, as their national dignity became
something very important to them. Realizing that the students'
appearance within at the school walls would reflect on the Kazakh

people as a whole, and keen not to let down the honour of the republic, Nazarbayev took it upon himself to work with those who were underachieving or lagging behind, maintaining order in the classroom and the dormitory, and preventing his compatriots, by persuasion and personal example, from behaving badly or inappropriately. Many of the Kazakh students were of shepherd-herding families from remote mountain villages, and didn't understand the Russian language, making it very difficult for them to study and impeding their performance. In these cases Nazarbayev volunteered to translate, earning him the gratitude and respect not only of his classmates but his teachers. His constructiveness, diligence and initiative were apparent in the way that, in the hot and deafening workshop in which they found themselves being trained, he was the first to gain the confidence to volunteer himself for the tasks set by their teachers. The boys were drawn to this informal leader and grouped themselves around him. Soon he was elected head of the group. His moral influence was such that a number of the more difficult students changed their outlook and became more positive.

Nazarbayev's leadership qualities manifested themselves on several different occasions while he was studying at the school. For example, in 1959 the famous Kazakh singer B.A. Tulegenova came as part of her tour to Dniprodzerzhynsk. Resolving to support his compatriot, Nazarbayev decided off his own bat to bring the upcoming performance to the attention of the plant workers and residents of the city. With the help of his fellow students, he quickly put up advertisements for it all across town. As a result, the hall in the city's Palace of Culture, where the concert took place, was packed. At the end of the performance, Nazarbayev took to the stage, handed the singer on behalf of his countrymen the huge bouquet of flowers for which they had pooled their resources, and warmly expressed his thanks.

A few months later came the second incident. At New Year there was a fracas involving some young Kazakh men who had got into a fight with some guests at a restaurant and been apprehended by the police. The situation was so serious that the possibility arose that all offenders might be sent home. It was Nazarbayev who went to bail them out. Thanks to his powers of rhetoric and persuasion the incident was settled with both parties fully reconciled.

One of the first to spot the clear makings of a leader in this talented, disciplined and purposeful young man was the master of the industrial training D.I. Pogorelov, who in informal conversation with his students,

Above:
Tempered with steel, Nazarbayev's fellow trainees in Ukraine, November 1958.

Opposite and below:
Album pictures.

assessing their abilities and prospects, openly predicted to each: 'You, my boy, will be an engineer, you a factory boss. For you, only prison awaits … But I see you, Nursultan, he said, becoming Chairman of the Council of Ministers.'

Prudent in his actions, reliable in matters of business and deeply honest in his dealings with people, Nazarbayev acquired a number of decent and loyal friends while studying at the school, friendships which lasted into later life. Amongst them were K.Z. Sarekenov, A. Abduramanov, A. Asanov, S.T. Ibragimov, K.M. Islamkulov, M.S. Narikbayev, M.B. Tatimov, and others, many of whom would go on to become first-rate specialist metallurgists, or prominent figures in public or political affairs.

The banks of the Dnieper had long been the home of a friendship between Nazarbayev and the Ukrainian boy Nikolay Litoshko, whose family all his whole life had treated him like a son. Leaving for his homeland, Nursultan invited his friend to come with him, and soon Nikolay found himself in what was for him a distant and unknown part of Kazakhstan. The friends worked side by side and lived together in their dormitory. But soon enough Nikolay was drafted into the army, after which their lives took very different paths. After nearly thirty years

Above:
Star work – Exemplary Worker.

Left:
Album picture.

Bottom:
Nursultan Nazarbayev –
a student of the Karaganda
Polytechnic Institute.

the two friends came across each other once more and on Nazarbayev's insistence Litoshko and his family finally made the upheaval to Kazakhstan, where they would be closer to one another.

It was during his final year at the school that disturbing rumours reached Nazarbayev about a crisis situation in Temirtau. Upon returning to Kazakhstan, he learnt from archival sources, and those who had witnessed the events before, that on 29 July 1959 there had been mass unrest amongst the townspeople, followed by riots, the arrival of troops, shooting and casualties. The main reason for what had happened in Temirtau was the contemptuous attitude of the state towards the working man, when building sites were being erected at a frenetic pace, and yet the workers were kept living in deplorable conditions, often without basic commodities and housing. The protest, in which thousands of workers and specialists participated, was brutally crushed, a curfew was declared in the city, and an investigation was carried out

to reveal the most active participants, six of whom were sentenced to the highest form of punishment – execution. Soon a taboo was placed on discussion of events, and the state tried for many decades to erase the memory of the rebellion. But the lessons Nursultan Nazarbayev learnt from the events in Temirtau in 1959 would stay with him for a long time.

A deep respect for the working man and the provision for him of a decent standard of living, as well as help for those without the means to care for themselves – the elderly, the disabled and children – contributed to Nazarbayev's philosophy of life which would go on to define his opinions on state policy. So it was that during the turbulent years of Perestroika at the end of the 1980s, and the hardest period of all during the establishment of independence and the global crises of 1997–98 and 2008–9, Nazarbayev, rather than dodging the practical difficulties,

Album picture. Fellow metal workers.

did everything in his power to address social issues and protect his people.

He would also constantly direct the free-market economy to those principles which had private business sharing in social responsibility alongside the state. He spoke of it as a valuable ally in tackling not only economic issues but social issues too. Corporate social responsibility, in his view, required the voluntary contribution of business to the development of society in its social, economic and ecological spheres. The state ought to be able to rely on this policy to create new jobs, guarantee the provision of social benefits to employees, and comply with environmental regulations.

The validity of Nazarbayev's position was to be evidenced by the tragic events of December 2011 in the city of Zhanaozen and the village of Shetpe in the Mangistau region. There a workers' dispute between state-sector companies and free-market businesses led to a spate of violence which left many dead and injured. The forces of law and order were at fault. The President immediately took personal control of the situation, dismissing the officials responsible, and setting up a government commission to investigate how the emergency had come about and how order could most quickly be restored in the city, before going to Zhanaozen to meet citizens in person. The overwhelming majority of the Kazakh people rallied around their leader in support.

On 13 April 1960, Nursultan Nazarbayev was for the second time awarded a certificate of merit by Dniprodzerzhynsk's Ukrainian Komsomol committee, again for training and participation in both social and Party sides of life in the school. On 26 April 1960, he graduated. It was decided by the examination committee that he would qualify as a second furnaceman of the eighth rank (in metallurgy, the highest rank one could achieve was tenth). Years later, he reflected on that period: 'Perhaps there is no institute of higher education that could have given me the training I received in my year and a half at Dniprodzerzhynsk. When I later went on to continue my studies of metallurgical sciences at an institute, I already understood practically everything. And if you add to this the practical skills I obtained in the four hours manufacturing work we did every day after class, then that confirms it.'

When he returned home after the conclusion of his studies, Nazarbayev awaited the opening of the plant and the chance to put to use the professional knowledge and skills he had acquired.

Sara Kunakayeva.

Nazarbayev and his bride.

Right:
Oh the Dnieper, how it roars and moans… The Dnieprostroi Dam.

Below:
The birth of the giant, where most Kazakhstan metal comes from – Karaganda's steelworks.

On 9 May 1960, by order No.616 of the Kazmetallurgstroy Trust, signed by its deputy manager I. Tkachenko, Nursultan Nazarbayev was the eighteenth Dniprodzerzhynsk alumnus to be taken on as a worker in the construction administration Domenstroy. The month and a half that he worked there as a concreter saw the completion of the blast furnace.

On the 27 June 1960, by order No.960 of the Kazmetallurgstroy, he was transferred to the Karaganda Metallurgical Plant for specialist work in the blast furnace, and on 1 July he was taken on as an ironworker on the casting machines of the plant's Grade 5 smelting workshop.

On 3 July 1960, on the eve of his twentieth birthday, Nazarbayev served as assistant furnaceman in the launch of the first and, at the time, the only blast furnace in Kazakhstan and Central Asia. Together with experts B.V. Yagovitov and K.P. Gerashenko, he played his part in the first ever smelting of iron in Kazakhstan. This date is remembered in history as the day that Kazakh Magnitka was born. So it was that the beginning of Nursultan Nazarbayev's working life coincided with a key moment in the life of the republic – the first successful operation of him who would one day be a leading figure in Kazakh metallurgy.

Those of Nazarbayev's Dniprodzerzhynsk classmates who also had the honour of participating in the first ever smelting were A. Abduramanov, D. Balmurzayev, S. Batyrkhanov, P. Zhanarbayev, M. Kistaubayev, T. Kurbanov, T. Kurmanbayev, A. Kyrykbayev, T. Orynbayev, A. Salimov, K. Sarekenov, A. Sokbekov, and J. Sultanbekov. Those who came to Temirtau to share the celebration of the workers' success with the builders and metallurgists were D.A. Kunayev, the First Secretary of the Kazakhstan Communist Party, the Chairman of the Council of Ministers of Soviet Kazakhstan J.A. Tashenev, the First Secretary of the Karaganda Regional Committee M.S. Solomentsev, and the leaders of the Party, Soviet and Komsomol bodies in the region and city of Temirtau.

Exactly half a century later, in July 2010, at the celebration of the fiftieth anniversary of Kazakh Magnitka, Nazarbayev again took part in the ceremonial anniversary smelting, where he personally presented state awards to many veterans of the companies with whom his own life's journey had begun. The country's highest award – the title of Hero of Labour – was awarded to a metallurgist renowned in Kazakhstan and honoured in the wider USSR, the steel founder A. Zhunusov, who had held his post at the furnace for more than half a century.

It is worth noting that the end of the 1950s and the beginning of the 1960s were marked for the Soviet people by the powerful spiritual and emotional revival connected with the Krushchev thaw in public and cultural life, by the totemic flight of the first man in space, Yuri Gagarin.

With it came building and construction work on an unprecedented scale. It all served to give the Soviet people a genuine pride in their country and demonstrate to them the advantages of the socialist system. Against this backdrop a film was released for the big screen which would become an anthem for young workers, M.M. Khutsiev's *Spring on Zarechnaya Street* with Nikolay Rybnikov in the main role. It was a

Above:

During break time. Nursultan Nazarbayev second from left, 1960.

heroic romanticization of the laborious work of the steelworker which would become a cult picture for generations of Soviet citizens. Unsurprisingly, this film was especially dear to the young metallurgist Nursultan, and its theme song became one of his personal favourites.

In August 1960, Nazarbayev was transferred to blast furnace No.1 as second furnaceman of the seventh class. A year later he was promoted to third furnaceman of the eighth class, and in February 1962 he had already progressed to second furnaceman of the nineth class, a rank held until February 1964.

He recalls in his book *Without Right and Left*: 'What kind of work is it that the furnaceman does? You have a heavy crowbar to crush the scrap, and a broad shovel to extract it. And there you are, in the depths of hell, the temperature about 2000 degrees. And then, of course, there's the gas and the dust. The work that these people have to do is awful. The metal emission process leaves no room for rest or complaint – you have no one to rely on but yourself. Skill is not enough: the metal often freezes, the worst accident of all. Then you have to climb, coated in asbestos, directly into the flames to pull out the broken equipment. Over the course of a shift you drink about half a bucket of salt water, and sweat about half of it straight back out. You get a cold shower after about half an hour's work. But if it's summer, you go out into the street,

and its 35 degrees out there too. The guys are exhausted the whole time, their muscles have no time to rest, and many get nosebleeds – everyone has their own physical response. Some cannot bear it and quit.'

But the truth is that this hellish work in the most extreme of conditions was at least handsomely paid, and soon Nazarbayev's salary had risen to 400 rubles, which at that time was on a par with that of a minister. Half his earnings he sent back to his parents, but, as he would later learn, they did not spend this money, setting it carefully aside in a savings account. When Nursultan got married, they returned every penny of it to him, to equip his young family for life. In December 1961, the young steelworker's dedication to his work was acknowledged for the first time with a decoration: he was honoured with the title of Shock Worker of Communist Labour.

However, despite the intense and gruelling work, Nazarbayev's energy and drive meant that he was unable to override the acute social problems which disrupted so many peoples lives. In *Without Right and Left*, he makes occasional mention of the harsh realities: 'We slept in an unheated dormitory where we huddled together for warmth on red, two-man bunks covered with mattresses. There was nowhere even to dry out our clothes, and so we would tend to leave our canvas overalls out in the frost, because they were easier to put on icy than soggy and

Doing one's duty with Komsomol enthusiasm.

heavy … The residential village was some way away, and no one had given any proper thought about how to bring people in to work. Every day, you would spend two hours just on the road. The dormitory was cold, you weren't getting enough sleep, and it was only your youth and physical strength that kept you going … Leisure time was out of the question, and the main entertainment we got were the mass brawls. There were murders and other critical exigencies every single day.'

Mindful of the sad events of 1959 in Temirtau and unable to stay on the sidelines any longer, Nazarbayev involved himself in public life almost without noticing it.

He gave a penetrating speech at the Tenth Congress of the Kazakh Komsomol, which took place on the 27–28 February 1962, and to which he had been sent as a delegate of the Karmetzavod Komsomol organization. In contrast to the majority of the speeches made at the Congress, the twenty-one-year-old Nazarbayev wasn't afraid to use his platform to bring up the issues troubling the young people of Kazakh Magnitka: 'The plant and the city of Temirtau are beset by problems, some of which we can resolve by ourselves, but many of which we cannot. One of these is the absence of any kind of cultural hub, where young people might spend their free time more healthily, and be encouraged towards artistic endeavour. We are not lacking in talent. We have all kinds of craftsmen but no arena for them to work in. On behalf of the young Communists of our city please help us to resolve this issue … We have many young people who are keen to be taught, but in our city they have no outlet.

'According to a government decree it was decided that a factory-VTUZ (higher technical education institution) would be built, but in two years all we have seen is a pile of papers, and so the problem remains. Neither the Ministry of Higher Education nor Gosplan (the State Planning Committee) nor the Komsomol Central Committee have taken the necessary measures to accelerate its construction. Komsomol members and the youth of Temirtau have long wanted a factory-VTUZ in their city and look with great hope to those with the power to make it so. It is time for it to happen … Why should not artistic luminaries come to us? It is rare for us to welcome any artists at all, like the poets and writers of Alma-Ata and other central cities where a cultural infrastructure is already in place. I would like one day to invite writers and poets to come and seek their heroic subjects among our people.

'And I have one more request. If you understand me correctly, we have a great number of young Kazakh men, but almost no Kazakh women. Therefore, on behalf of my friends, I appeal to women – to female medics, teachers, or construction workers – to come and join us at Kazakh Magnitka, where there is proper work for every one of you, and we could all be very happy.'

This was followed by loud applause and laughter in the hall.

Exactly two months later, on 16–20 April 1962, Nazarbayev, accompanied by the Secretary of the Komsomol Karmetzavod Committee, R. Gibadullin, and the head of the Stalstroy directorate, V. Mikhno, was sent as the Kazakh delegate to the Fourteenth Komsomol Congress, where he represented the Komsomol members and young people of Temirtau. At that same congress, he was elected as a candidate for membership of the Komsomol Central Committee. In 1962, the young metallurgist was awarded certificates of distinction by the Supreme Council of Soviet Kazakhstan, and by the Komsomol Central Committee.

Documents from those years go some way to showing how it was that a simple working man came to rise through the ranks so quickly. For example, in the report of the First Secretary of the Karaganda Regional Komsomol Committee's second assembly on 28 May 1962, in a document summarizing the results of socialist competition amongst the Komsomol youth teams, we read: 'In March of this year, the Komsomol Committee of the Kazmetallurgy Trust organized for its young Komsomol collectives a relay race with the motto "The Fourteenth Congress of the Young Communist League – Celebrating Youthful Energy". Around 200 Komsomol youth teams entered the socialist competition to complete the five-month plan by the opening day of the Komsomol Congress. The result was that more than 5000 young builders of Kazakh Magnitka had completed it by 1 April … The competitions between the brigades and the Shock Workers of Communist Labour, and the political work that was carried out at the same time, was to have a positive effect on these young people. Numerous examples among the young Shock Workers bear witness to this. Such as, indeed, Nursultan Nazarbayev, who, within a year of leaving his village for Kazakh Magnitka had mastered the task of the blast furnaceman. When Magnitka produced its first cast iron, it was Nazarbayev who was at the furnace. In eight months he had been promoted twice and become the second furnaceman of the largest steel plant.

The Karaganda Socialist journal of 1962 – article on Blast Furnace No. 2 of Karmetplant.

'By now he was much more than an iron-smelter – he was a public figure. There were hundreds and thousands of young people on hand with the moral qualities to serve as an example to be followed. Komsomol ought to promote their cause more widely.'

Nazarbayev's attainment did not go unnoticed. Articles about him, and photos of him in his uniform felt hat, were appearing with enviable regularity in newspapers such as *Kazakh Truth*, *Socialist Karaganda*, *Industrial Karaganda*, *The Karaganda Communist* and *Temirtau's Worker*.

Nazarbayev was given further encouragement when he was sent on the first expedition abroad between 27 July and 5 August 1962. He was part of the Soviet delegation that took part in the eighth World Festival of Youth and Students in the Finnish capital of Helsinki, which brought together representatives from over a hundred countries from all continents. The festival's programme included numerous plenary sessions, working meetings, seminars and debates. Nazarbayev and the other Soviet delegates gladly took part in these proceedings, allowing them to meet with their foreign counterparts. There was a noteworthy dispute between the Soviet and American participants about the benefits of communism and capitalism. Nazarbayev, in his characteristic energetic and assertive style, took part. Hearing so professional and well-argued a speech, backed up by facts and figures, the opposition were ready to question whether he could be a mere worker. Nazarbayev held out his calloused hands.

At the same festival one other momentous meeting took place – with the first cosmonaut Yuri Gagarin. The newspaper *Komsomol Truth* promptly published a photo report. The day before, the young delegate from Kazakhstan had been presented with a Komsomol badge which had travelled into space with another Soviet cosmonaut, V.F. Bykovsky.

Nazarbayev's senior Communist workmates couldn't help but keep an eye on this exemplary worker and emerging figure. On 13 October 1961, at a meeting of the Temirtau city council, as recommended by the senior workers and factory veterans B.V. Yagovitov and V.K. Veretennikov, and decided by the primary Party group of the Karmetzavod blast furnace, it was agreed that Nazarbayev would stand as a candidate for Communist Party membership.

On 15 November 1962, his one-year probationary period came to an end, and, on the recommendation of V.K. Veretennikov, A.A. Rybin, and T.A. Likhomanov, the Karmetzavod primary Party group accepted Nazarbayev as a CP member. This decision was confirmed on 14 February 1963 by the assembled town committee, and Nursultan

Certificate of merit from the Soviet Committee at the eighth World Festival of Youth and Students.

Young people from all over the world with Yuri Gagarin, during the eighth World Festival of Youth and Students.

Nazarbayev was awarded Party number 11054052 (later 02637097), which he would hold right up until August 1991, when after the infamous events of the anticonstitutional August Putsch he took the difficult decision to leave the Party.

The year 1962 turned out to be eventful for Nazarbayev. No sooner was he back from the Festival of Youth than he had started a family, having married Karaganda-born Sara Alpysovna Kunakayeva, who worked as a controller at Karmetzavod. As was customary at the time, they had a small but merry Komsomol youth wedding on 25 August, in the modest Komsomolets Cafe with a circle of close friends, colleagues and relatives. They went on to have three daughters – Dariga (born 1963), Dinara (1967), and Alia (1980).

The same year Nazarbayev started at college. Accustomed from childhood to do nothing by halves, he decided to build on his professional skills and theoretical knowledge. Moving on from plant in September 1962, he studied metallurgy at the Temirtau branch of the Karaganda Polytechnic Institute, specializing in ferrous metals, a course to learn on the job. From February 1964, wholly dedicated to his studies, he was training full-time.

ID card of a member of the Communist Party of the Soviet Union.

In August 1965, ending the third year of the course, the Institute's metallurgical faculty closed. Nazarbayev transferred to Karmetzavods recently opened Factory-VTUZ, where he continued his studies at evening classes. Meanwhile he started work as a manager of the plant's blast furnace. In August 1966 he became the furnaces gasman and, a little later, its senior gasman.

In July 1967 Nazarbayev finished at Factory-VTUZ. The state examination committee decided that, alongside his diploma (No.367782), he qualified as an Engineer-Metallurgist. Graduating with him of his Karmetzavod colleagues were V.F. Kolbasa, K.O. Omashev, J. Askeev, T. Iskakov, amongst others. Meanwhile, Narzarbayev's public profile continued to grow further and further.

On 17 July 1968, at a review and election meeting of the primary Party group of the blast furnace, he was elected as a Party member for his workshop. On 20 November he then became its Party Secretary. Not that he broke his ties with the Komsomol. On 21 October 1968 he took part in the plenum of the Komsomol Central Committee in Moscow, the fiftieth anniversary of the Leninist Komsomol. Exactly a year before, on 31 October 1967, it had been decided by the Central Committee that he, as a Shock Worker of Communist Labour, proposer of the challenge to economize fuel usage, and Chairman of the Komsomol Spotlight headquarters, would be one of the first to receive one of the Komsomol Medals of Honour which had been introduced on 28 March 1966.

But despite his early public recognition, he did not make an automatic transition to Komsomol and Soviet work on a professional basis. Engrossed in his work and aware of his worth as a self-reliant specialist, this was not what he initially aspired to. This explains the fact that when the First Secretary of the Temirtau City Committee, L. Katkov, proposed to Nazarbayev that he become the head of the city's Komsomol body, his reply was a categorical refusal: 'This city needs more metallurgists…' There were also material considerations: the salary of the First Party Secretary was potentially less than the salary of a senior gasman, and Nazarbayev needed to make good money to support his family, which now included two daughters of school-going age, and to help his parents still caring for his younger brothers and a sister.

Party leaders decided to punish him for his disobedience, and called a committee meeting where he was accused of political immaturity and cowardice and reprimanded with the removal of his CPSU card, at the time a severe punishment which could lead to all kinds of misfortune. Nazarbayev was forced to fight for his reputation and his future, for which it was said, everything on the line.

Being a candidate member for the Central Committee of the Young Communist League, he decided to make a direct appeal to the Committee's First Secretary, S. Pavlov. To his relief, he managed not

Nazarbayev – a student of Karaganda Polytechnic.

International Workers' Day – Nazarbayev leads the parade for the Karaganda Metallurgical Plant during the 1 May celebrations. Termitau, 1964.

only to get through, but to explain the situation fully. In the end, at a meeting of the parent body, the Karaganda Regional Party Committee, the decision of the Temirtau City Party Committee was reversed, and a penalty instead imposed on the First Secretary – for taking the wrong approach to recruitment.

That incident served as a lesson. Rather than weaken Nazarbayev's social position, it strengthened it: it so happened that in 1968 he was awarded the title of Outstanding Soviet Student of Metallurgy, and in March 1969 he was elected to the twelfth convocation of the Temirtau City Council deputies.

In June 1969 he was sent abroad once again: he made a tourist visit to the Czechoslovak Socialist Republic. The tour programme was intense and, as well as the historical and cultural sights he saw, Nursultan Nazarbayev was part of the group of Kazakh envoys invited by the Central Czechoslovak Trade Union Committee who had friendly meetings with the working people of Czechoslovakia, as Karaganda regional radio stations and local newspapers were to report. But for him personally, this trip was important. It took place after Soviet troops had brutally crushed the Prague Spring in August 1968. It enabled him to compare the quality of life in Czechoslovakia with that in his homeland.

By the summer of 1969, the new First Secretary of the Temirtau City Party Committee, N.G. Davydov, invited Nazarbayev to lead the Department for Industry and Transport. There was a sharply pragmatic calculation behind this: it was vital for Party and government bodies to focus on galvanizing the State District Power Plant 1 and Thermoelectric Plant 1 of the Karmetzavod, and to accelerate the commissioning of an oxygen-converting station, the 250-tonne converters, at a time when no metallurgical enterprise in the Soviet Union had any of more than 100-tonne converters.

Known by sight and name, not just to the managers and key personnel but to most of the ordinary workers, well versed in industrial and technological infrastructure and exercising authority over a workforce who trusted him, Nazarbayev could not have been more suited.

Nazarbayev took advice from friends in the factory. This time he did not refuse. On 9 July 1969, at the meeting of the Temirtau City Party Committee, he was welcomed into office. He worked at this post for six months and coped admirably. As early as the customary anniversary of the October Revolution, the plant workers were reporting back advance. Soon enough, the oxygen-converter was being erected, and the goal was in sight.

Such was his success that at the end of 1969 he found himself given an altogether new role. On the eve of the one-hundredth anniversary of the birth of Lenin, founder of the Communist Party and the Soviet state, it was decided that every company, institution and organization in the Soviet Union, without exception, would organize their labour collectives to come together for a celebration. The people of Temirtau were called upon for a sharp increase in the ideological and political education among the general population, especially the young. This called for effective organizers. Once again, Nazarbayev was chosen.

On 20 December 1969, at the Plenum of the Temirtau Komsomol, he was elected and confirmed as First Secretary. Thus on 9 January 1970 the Temirtau City Party Committee relieved him of his duties as head of the Department for Transport and Industry. Nazarbayev would serve as First Secretary of the city's Komsomol operations until June 1971. During this period, he would go on to participate as the Karaganda delegate in the Twelfth Komsomol Congress of Kazakhstan (11–12

Song helps us to work and live – in a moment of leisure.

Standing on the podium of the Twelfth Komsomol Congress of Kazakhstan, the First Secretary of the Temirtau Komsomol, Nursultan Nazarbayev. Alma-Ata, 11 March 1970.

March 1970), where he would be promoted to a member of the Komsomol Central Committee of Kazakhstan.

Overall, 1969 was a turning point in the life of the twenty-nine-year-old Nursultan, and an important landmark in his career. He went from being a worker to a one with real managerial authority, actively involved in Komsomol Party business. However, he had not become cut off from the working world; he merely found himself dealing with its problems from a position of higher, and more widespread, political responsibility, overseeing them from his position as a Party member and guide. Even decades later, as President of the whole country, it was common for him to be seen wearing workman's overalls, visiting industrial centres and construction sites, and talking to directors, engineers and workers with a full grasp of what they were doing.

The scale of economic development is evident from the report Nazarbayev made on 3 July 1970 at the Third Plenum of the Kazakh Komsomol. The report covered the construction and start-up of the Karmet oxygen converter; the creation of new housing and cultural facilities; the encouragement of young people towards technical creativity, rationalization and invention; the expansion of production training, and the increase of those workers becoming fully qualified; the participation of young workers and students in stations for the maintenance of law and order; and the fight against theft.

With its new powers, the Karaganda Metallurgical Kombinat significantly expanded the range of its output, producing pig iron, coke, open hearth and converter steel, slabs and coils of hot-rolled steel.

Further to heighten production, the plant was reorganized to incorporate the Kazakh steel plant and the Atasusk and South Toparsk arms of the Alekseevsky dolomite mine.

In 1970 Nazarbayev was one of those senior production workers and persons of the republic to be awarded with a medal For Valiant Labour, in Commemoration of the One-hundredth Anniversary of Lenin's Birth.

Nazarbayev was operating on a regional and indeed national level. In 1970, in preparation for the plenum of the Sixth Temirtau Komsomol, he proposed answering the call of the Hero of Socialist Labour P.L. Lisovenko for economy of working time with an initiative for Achievement Within Seven Hours. Led by the officials V. Gushin (the Spetspromsroy head) and N. Nurgaliev (the Stalstroy head), this initiative was taken up by all the Komsomol organizations of Soviet Kazakhstan, and became known as Kazakhstan's Hour.

That same year, Nazarbayev organized specific help for patron farms in the Nurinsky district during that spring's field work. For the harvest in the autumn he provided 200 tractors, 300 combines and 300 drivers. Fourteen training points were put together in Temirtau, where 610 mechanics undertook acceleration courses. These cases are a testimony not only to Nazarbayev's innovative instincts but to his know-how and entrepreneurial flair, enabling him to find solutions which benefited the common interests of a wide range of skills.

The Soviet adage 'everything hangs on who's working for you' was not lost on Nazarbayev. His foremost professional imperative had become the efficiency with which his men were selected, trained and assigned. The archives have preserved the names of many members of the Temirtau Komsomol with whom Nazarbayev worked closely, and with whom he grew up. Among them were the Party Secretaries V. Kachura, M. Lebedenko, and M. Pauli, the Committee workers Y. Korobov, D. Maksimovskaya, the writer of the newspaper *Temirtau's Worker* Y. Vetkalo, the city council worker B. Zhakupov, the tailor V. Kindishov, the student V. Kramarev, the department worker E. Ryzhenkov, the Secretaries of the primary Komsomol organizations F. Bisembayeva, O. Bryukhanova, V. Efteeva, L. Zaribov, P. Klimov, V. Manin, A.S. Nekrasov, O. Pridelina, S. Radchenko, P. Ramazanov, K. Simashkov, T. Suleymenov, N. Tretyavok, and L. Fentsel, and many more. The majority of recommendations for Komsomol admission, and decisions concerning material and moral incentives for distinguished workers, bore Nazarbayev's signature.

The heart of Kazakh Magnitka.

It was Nazarbayev's civic maturity, no less than his professional competence and aptitude for business, that year after year extended his fame and promoted him through the official channels over to higher positions. The state took a special interest in how potential everywhere was being fulfilled, attributable to energetic young leaders, capable of working with dedication across a range of voters. The scruple with which Nazarbayev conducted his professional relationships would in the end come to determine his own personal status. So it was that he found himself with a new promotion, when on 10 June 1971 he was elected Second Secretary of the Temirtau Party Committee.

Nazarbayev's role was to oversee the fields of industry and generation of capital. However, the actual range of his work far outstripped the scope of his duties. During those two and a half years he was involved in every aspect of the city's social and economic life, as evidenced by the themes of his speeches and the decisions and documents on which he worked: the training of workers in industrial and construction companies, the effectiveness and safety of transportation, the creation of reserves and of economic regimes, the quality of food for the workers, everyday consumer services, the provision of power to the industrial and civil facilities, the construction of housing, cultural and entertainment institutions, patronal support and so on. Nazarbayev was also the head of the political staff for the construction of the Karaganda Metallurgical Kombinat. He would often disappear for days on a construction site. It was this period that saw built the mechanical workstations, the expanded thermoelectric plants, and a whole network of railways.

Karaganda's workforce rally on launching the rolled steel mill.

3

Secretary of the Party Committee

It was on 20 October 1973 that, by the recommendation of the First Secretary of the Karaganda Regional Committee Party V.K. Akulintseva, Nursultan Nazarbayev was accepted for the post of Secretary of the Party Committee of the Karaganda Metallurgical Plant, where he would work until March 1977. In those years the staff of the plant numbered more than 30,000 people. Of that number, the Party organization comprised 2,500 Communists.

His chief mission in the new post was to find solutions to problems connected with a drop in production and the frequency of accidents on the factory complex, amid other related unfortunate incidents. Even in January 1972, the incumbent secretary of the Temirtau Town Party anxiously noted serious shortfalls at the *Parthozaktiv* (Party economic staff) meeting in Temirtau, revolving around the organization of production.

'For the First of May holiday – the reward for our labour.'
A meeting for the launch of Blast Furnace No. 4. Temirtau,
1 May 1975 (displaying Lenin's portrait).

The factory's production potential was not being fully utilized: expensive equipment was often left unused for long periods, and frequent accidents and disruption on the production line were taking place, which led to a low quality of product, limited stock, and a systematic failure to deliver to consumers. In 1971 there were eighty-one accidents on the plants, as a result of which 80,000 tonnes of scrap metal, 48,400 tonnes of steel, 87,000 tonnes of rolled metal, as well as many other products were wasted.

The ongoing complications were largely linked to the high fluctuation in staff numbers, leading to a lack of basic living and work conditions, and a corresponding low level of qualification amongst the overwhelming majority of the engineers and workers at the plant.

Through Nursultan Nazarbayev's insistence, a special plan was launched to increase the levels of preparation and boost the qualification levels of the staff on the plant. This led to the opening of an evening technical college to provide education in a number of specializations (agricultural production, converter and open-hearth steel production, rolled steel production, mechanical equipment installation of metallurgical workshops, electrical equipment installation, lifting-transport machinery) with space for 300 people, and also a branch of the Moscow Institute for Advanced Studies for Professional and Management Training for fifty people.

With the arrival of Nazarbayev's reliable methods, there began weekly meetings with factory workers where managers of the plant, the Party committee, professional committee and Komsomol all took part. They wasted no time in the workshops and, without unnecessary formalities, dealt with issues related to production and other current problems. There and then they took the appropriate steps. Thanks to these *letuchkas*, many valuable innovations and logical reforms were made at the factory, allowing the effective resolution of an entire range of serious production problems.

At the same time, the Secretary of the Party Committee also had to concern himself with social matters. These included the construction of living spaces, health clinics, kindergartens and crèches, sport-health centres, and cultural facilities amongst others.

The originality, complexity and sense of responsibility of the young Party secretary meant he demanded of himself that he increased his theoretical knowledge and knowledge of political instrumentation. He began the attainment of a higher level of qualification without taking a break from the factory. In 1973, Nazarbayev, on the decision of the

Nazarbayev's portrait on joining the Extramural Higher Party School of the CPSU.

Temirtau – the Kazakh name means 'iron mountain'.

Temirtau City Party Committee, entered into a three-year extramural study course at the Higher Party School of the CPSU – one of the few educational establishments in the USSR where it was possible to receive the highest political and management qualification in the country. This he successfully completed in 1976.

Between them, despite all the efforts of the directors and Party committee of the Karmetplant (Karaganda Metallurgical Plant), it did not appear possible to unravel such a knot of problems as accumulated spontaneously in the business. By and large these mistakes were systemic in nature because of allowances made by departments of the Council of Ministers in the design process, and the building and planning work for the metallurgical complex. Repairing these blunders was possible only at the most senior level, since all crucial solutions were made exclusively at that level.

Grasping this, together with the director of the plant O.I. Tishchenko, Nazarbayev tried persistently to evoke a response from the republic and union power structures and to bring to their attention the worsening situation at the metallurgical giant. To quote: 'I would like to draw attention to the need for resolution of a number of matters, which depend on the union and republic bodies. For a number of years the Ministry of the Iron and Steel Industry of the USSR have developed

Left:
The building of the Karaganda Regional Party. Karaganda, 1970s.

Below:
Nazarbayev at his administration desk.

the plant without any precise targets in mind, allowing serious failure in meeting objectives, which has lead to the creation of financial irregularities.

'As a result the development of the mining base, the energy plant and its repair services has been sacrificed, so there was poor quality technical equipment and automation of several production processes.'

Nazarbayev's memorandum gave a frank picture of the real state of affairs on the Kazakhstan Magnitogorsk site. Minchermeta – the Ministry of Ferrous Metallurgy – ignored Nazarbayev's report, so he directed the letter to the Secretary of the Central Committee of the CPSU, V.I. Dolgikh, himself a professional metallurgist who had for many years run the Norilsk Mountain metallurgical plant, and knew the specifics of the industry first hand.

In the end, the insistence of the new Party secretary was rewarded. In the summer of 1974, a state commission arrived at the Karmetkombinat, comprising representatives from the Council of Ministers, headed by V.I. Dolgikh.

After a few months, arising from the work of the commission, Nursultan Nazarbayev was called to Moscow for recognition before an important ideologue of the Communist Party of the Soviet Union – the Secretary of the Central Committee of the CPSU, Mikhail Suslov. As a result, the Secretariat released a decree on 12 December 1974 entitled 'Regarding the Work of the Temirtau City Plant in Strengthening Working-technological Discipline, and Bettering Production and Living

Album pictures.

Conditions of the Workers on the Plant'. Later the Council of Ministers of the USSR made a decision to guarantee the yearly provision of 80,000 square metres of housing in Temirtau, as well as the construction of two kindergartens for 1,660 children, two professional-technical colleges, a metallurgical technical college, engineering colleges, Palaces of Culture, a stadium holding 15,000 people, a swimming pool, a health centre, as well as leisure centres on the right bank of the Samarkand reservoir and other amenities.

Later in his book *In the Heart of Eurasia*, Nursultan Nazarbayev gratefully recalled those years during the construction boom in Temirtau. It was especially then, according to him, that in many ways he had his first experience of construction of important collective sites, which would prove advantageous to him in the building of the new capital of Kazakhstan, Astana.

In February 1976, Nazarbayev spoke as a delegate with elected representatives at the Fourteenth Congress of the Communist Party of Kazakhstan. He briefed the leaders of the republic and the other congress members in detail of the measures taken by the Party Committee to ensure the speedy recovery of metallurgical units, heightening their technical capabilities and efficiency, and bettering the quality of production.

By this time two powerful blast furnaces, two '1700 converters' for sheets of cold rolled metal, a powerful thermal power station and the No. 2 agricultural factory complex had been installed on the site, among many other facilities of high importance. Soon thereafter, the initiation of the Aglomer operation was planned, as well as the installation of coke-oven battery No. 7, sheet and curved metal

Album picture.

workshops, and a range of other production processes. After that, social matters were addressed.

These successes were all the more valuable being, as they were, achieved despite formidable pressure. Literally every step of the way was blocked by multiple obstacles. Devoted to the Karmetkombinat, his local company, with heartfelt loyalty, at the end of 1976, in an extraordinary intervention, Nursultan Nazarbayev decided to criticize bitterly the running of the Union of Industrial Ministries and the highest ranking divisional leaders. In an article entitled 'Ranked as a laggard. What is interfering with the good work of the Karaganda Metallurgical Plant?' – taken from a page of *Pravda* (True), the official daily paper of the Soviet Union printed by a division of the CPSU – published on 29 December 1976, he rebuked these bodies, citing facts of bureaucracy, red-tape and a negligent attitude to business affairs on their part.

Specifically in this period came the first shoots of awareness that the problems lay deeper than he had supposed in the planned economic system itself. They lay with the principles of administrative command, the rigid centralization of economic life – a resentment that grew in the consciousness of the young Party secretary.

Three and a half stressful years working in the post of Karmet Party Secretary did not pass without great effort. Everyone talked about the fact that the initiative, drive, organizational talent and absolute focus of this man proved to be of essential value on the broadest scale.

In March 1977, Nazarbayev was chosen as Secretary of the Karaganda Regional Party for Industry. Already, by December of that year, he had risen to the Second Secretary. Now amongst his duties, along with overseeing the ferrous metallurgical plant, there fell to him the coordination of industries such as coal, light metallurgy, energy and mechanical engineering. Studying the coalmining industries in the region, Nazarbayev focused on increasing the output of coal mines, which had lagged compared to the spectacular growth of the metallurgy and energy industries and had not been able to adapt with alacrity to the increased demand for coal. Swiftly confronting the worsening situation, he assembled a large group of students and specialists. With them he oversaw the maximizing of production on the part of Karaganda-ugol (the Karaganda coal mining plant). Thus began the reclaiming of the Borlin and Shubarkol coalfields through sound management.

Another vivid scar on coal production was the unacceptably high accident rate for the miners. One of the most tragic events was the catastrophe of February 1978 on the Sokurskaya mine, taking the lives of seventy-three miners. In response, he took matters concerning safety and work conditions for miners into his own hands, himself

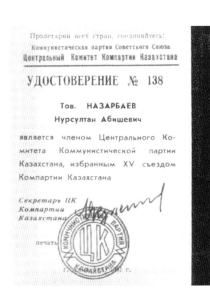

Nazarbayev's pass card as a member of the Central Committee of the Communist Party of Kazakhstan.

Left:
Certificate of attendance at the
Extramural Higher Party School
of the CPSU.

Below:
Nazarbayev's critical article
in *Pravda* – the daily newspaper
of the Soviet Union – entitled
'From a Position of Reason and
Fairness', 27 December 1976.

going down to the most dangerous and accident prone shafts on frequent occasions and acquainting himself with the situation on site.

Thanks to his commitment, these life-and-death matters began to ease. Meanwhile, most mining families lived in barracks, shared flats and even peasant huts. The Regional Secretary managed to get decree No. 211. approved by the Council of Ministers of the USSR, 'Concerning Measures for the Long-term Development of Town Accommodation and the Betterment of Everyday Living Conditions of the People of the Towns and Villages of the Karaganda Region'. It was effective from 6 March 1980. This was an important move by the USSR government, giving a widely noted kick-start to the construction of the mining capital and, consequently, to the development of the Karaganda region. The specific achievements during the 1970s in Karaganda were the construction of many homes for mine workers, improved engineering logistics, and the significant increase in the output of the TPP (Thermal Power Station).

In 1977, Nazarbayev's family suffered a heavy loss; at the age of seventy-two the dearly loved mother Alzhan Zhatkanbaykyzy Nazarbayev passed away. However, not long before this, Nursultan had brought his mother back to their home village. Throughout his life he was to feel sorrow that he had not been lucky enough to be by his 'Zheneshe' in her final hours. He was unreservedly her favourite, as the firstborn.

In December 1979, Nursultan would become Secretary of the Central Committee of the Communist Party of Kazakhstan for Industry, Transport and Infrastructure. To all intents and purposes, he was now one of the principal leaders of the republic.

Regarding Nazarbayev's experience of industry and management accumulated over his time working at a major industrial centre, his progress was seen as entirely logical and predictable. He had done everything properly on his part, and the specific sense of mutual

Temirtau, Metallurgists'
Prospect, 1970.

understanding between Nazarbayev and the First Secretary of the
Central Committee of the Communist Party of Kazakhstan,
Dinmukhamed Kunayev, deriving from the similarity in their
professional careers. Both were brought up in the field of industrial
labour, both were metallurgists, both honed their craft at the Central
Kazakhstan giant complex.

With his family home established in Alma-Ata, he spent many years
working and living in Temirtau and the Karaganda region, of which
he would always speak with special warmth. 'Temirtau is, for me, a
cradle,' he has said. 'The story of Magnitogorsk, the story of Temirtau,
the fate of its people is inseparable from my own fate. If Magnitogorsk
and Temirtau had not been in my life, I never would have become
President.'

It was telling that in his first important work – the book *Steel Profile
of Kazakhstan*, published in 1985 – he spoke in lofty terms of the
Karaganda Metallurgical plant, the history of its installation and
development, its transformation into a multinational workplace, its role
as a platform for creative ideas and initiative on the part of the workers
in the plant.

It says a lot that when, in April 1990, Nursultan Nazarbayev
became President of the Kazakh SSR, his first trip in the new role was
to Temirtau.

Nazarbayev worked as Secretary of the Central Committee of the
Communist Party of Kazakh SSR for more than four years. He devoted

this period to strengthening the industrial potential of Kazakhstan in, above all, the development of the oil, gas and chemical industries, and in mechanical engineering and production of consumer goods. He was not afraid to pose difficult questions to the Bureau of the Central Committee of the Communist Party of Kazakhstan, to the Central Committee of the CPSU or, indeed, to the Council of Ministers of the USSR, while remaining compliant with their decisions. Gradually he gained recognition as one of the most influential and business-savvy leaders of the republic. His work was also recognized with the distinguished award of the Order of the Red Banner of Labour.

Besides his macro-scale deliberations, he did not overlook the small-scale concerns of the common citizen. Archive documents bear witness to the fact that in 1980–81, in his role as deputy of the Supreme Council of the Kazakh SSR, at the tenth assembly for the Kostogan electoral district of the Merkenskiy district of the Zhambyl region, Nazarbayev fulfilled the mandate of his electorate by securing an irrigation structure for the village of Merka, a House of Culture on the collective farm named Victory, and a filling station on the Shyganak site. For the time, this was an act of some daring; as a rule building even small structures on a regional level did not occur without permission from Moscow and the backing of the regional administration.

During the same period, in February 1981, Nursultan Nazarbayev was to become deputy of the Supreme Council of the USSR and a member of the Central Revisionary Commission of the CPSU – an organ concerned with checking the finances of the Party departments.

By the start of the 1980s the steel industry in the Soviet Union was showing signs of stagnation, affecting practically all sides of life. A damaged economy was having its effect. Benefits may have been flowing from the yearly completion of a large quantity of major industrial and social objectives and a rising standard of life, but the rate of economic growth persistently fell.

The roots of the problem lay, fundamentally, in the inert Soviet economy. It was built on strictly centralized administrative-command directives. But in the context of a dawning post-industrialized world in the 1970s and 1980s, economic expansion lagged far behind the leading countries of the world in technological terms.

Most post-industrial economies were prioritizing development of the hi-tech sectors like microelectronics, software, telecommunications, robot technology and biotechnology. The Soviet bloc was concerning itself with mining and heavy industry. Its view of the form its national

Kazakhstan Communist Party headquarters in the 1980s.

economy should take harked back to a wartime industrial complex. Exaggerating the significance of the Cold War with the West came to dominate and the industrial scene and take up colossal resources.

The Soviet economy was vulnerable. It was orientated towards maximizing production at the expense of innovation and an adaptable pool of labour. Industry equipment was virtually not renewed and was proving physically and morally wearing for the work teams. The pace at which methods of mechanization and automation were introduced was sluggardly. By the 1980s, manual labour engaged nearly 50 million: roughly a third in industry, more than half in construction, and a quarter in village farming.

Typically, production was inefficient, the quality of work low, products poorly made, and an imbalance between production and demand. The dominant production was in heavy industry, comprising a quarter of GDP. A consequence was a chronic deficit of food and consumer goods.

Grief from the Soviet economic deadlock was delayed by the unexpected descent of the golden rain from oil money. The impact in the world of the massive energy crisis of 1973 led to a sharp jump in the price of oil. Exports started to create huge incomes from oil, facilitating the importation of mass consumer goods. Most products required oil, creating the illusion that the economy was safe.

However, what was urgently required was economic restructuring towards the hi-tech, along with the equally pivotal modernization of industrial equipment and the raising of conditions of work through innovative technology. Dependence on exporting natural resources eventually compounded the negative situation in the economy. This time of stagnation was referred to as the time of missed opportunities.

Bureaucratic bodies multiplied. Inner Party-economic nomenclature morphed into a privileged class of their own. There was a crisis in the state ideology, which day by day grew more remote from what was practised in reality. There emerged a dissident movement.

As a result, towards the start of the 1980s, Soviet society surreptitiously lived with a presentiment of change, in need of economic reform, the democratization of political life and an end to the international isolation that characterized the Soviet Union. This urgent demand was for higher state officials to become 'Soldiers of the Party', for the highly educated and experienced technocrats to come to power, ruling not by abstract ideological axioms but in the true interests of the people.

Such were, objectively, the deepest reasons behind Nursultan Nazarbayev's emergence as the head of government of the Kazakh Soviet Socialist Republic.

A photo from the album. The dromedary camel remains a feature of traditional life in south-west Kazakhstan.

4

The Moment of Truth

On 22 March 1984, at the age of forty-three, Nazarbayev was appointed Chairman of the Council of Ministers of the Kazakh SSR, becoming the youngest prime minister of any of the constituent republics of the USSR.

His arrival as head of government coincided with the start of Perestroika (restructure) in the Soviet Union. The new General Secretary Mikhail Gorbachev's announcement of the start of Perestroika, Glasnost (openness) and Acceleration was greeted by Nazarbayev, and the entire nation, with huge enthusiasm as a signal of a fresh epoch and new departures.

The peaceful demonstration of 16 December 1986, with its popular appeal for true autonomy, was suppressed – but heralded independence for Kazakhstan.

Not long before his appointment, Nazarbayev had arranged a significant meeting with Gorbachev.

'What do you think? Have you got the backbone for this?' asked Gorbachev.

'This is a difficult time,' he went on. 'There will be panic, there will be upheaval...'

The announcement of the concept of Perestroika, in terms of restructuring the economy for efficiency, was to introduce market elements, transparency in government decisions, self-motivated enterprise and the expansion of the rights of the labour force.

The power of local governments would be strengthened by them genuinely fulfilling their own aims. It was apt that Nursultan Nazarbayev's world view had been formed in the 1960s, during Krushchev's thaw. He was not a novice but an experienced manager, well familiar with political structuring and the actual state of affairs in the Soviet economy.

Nursultan Nazarbayev analyzed the situation across industry: village agriculture, transport, the service industry, social welfare, culture, education and science. He became vividly aware of an extreme 'liberality with the truth' in the difference between official propaganda and

Mikhail Gorbachev (left) was to regard Nursultan Nazarbayev as a potential successor.

СОВЕТ МИНИСТРОВ СССР

УДОСТОВЕРЕНИЕ № 0053

Тов. НАЗАРБАЕВ

Нурсултан Абишевич

является Председателем
Совета Министров Казахской ССР

Председатель Совета Министров СССР
Управделами Совета Министров СССР
Москва, Кремль. 1985 г.

Совет Министров СССР

№ 0053

Above:
The promulgation of Nazarbayev's charimanship of the Council of Ministers of the Kazakh SSR was issued in 1985.

Below:
The building of the Council of Ministers of the Kazakh SSR. Alma-Ata, in the 1980s.

statistical accuracy. More emphatically than ever he came to see the necessity of measures to ensure a speedy changeover to a new type of economy.

Kazakhstan was especially beset by the complexity of the ineffectual structuring of industry. Kazakhstan had been given the role of provider of basic goods in the USSR national economy, leaving it with an imbalance between mining and the production of consumer goods. Also, industry debt was lower than average in the Soviet Union.

As a consequence, the republic produced two-thirds of the USSR's light metals and light metal composites, three-quarters of coal and ferrous metal ore, more than 90 per cent of crude oil, almost half of all grain, one-third of its meat and more than 20 per cent of wool, and doing so at unjustifiably low prices. At the same time, Kazakhstan had been obliged to produce up to 95 per cent of equipment for light industry and precious metal transportation, two-thirds of metal-cutting machines, 45 per cent of wool and cotton fabrics, all of the automobile industry, agriculture, everyday technology, and the majority of consumer goods. As a result, due to this disproportionate exchange of resources, Kazakhstan was in the demeaning position of being a subsidized republic.

Nazarbayev was actively attentive to these problems during stewardship under the Soviet structure. He was also alert to sharp contrast between the city and countryside. His official notes from 1984 record the fact that by 1984 the construction of state farms comprised 49 per cent; that more than a quarter of farm employees were in need of accommodation; and that the total amount of village children in preschool departments was no higher than 36 per cent.

The pace of growth of production and industrial output in the republic was somewhat lower than planned. Production quotas were not being met quarterly. Return on capital investment was falling. From more than 300 industrial centres registered in the previous ten years, almost half did not reach their output potential. Village agriculture had run up debt in terms of grain and animal products and at the state and collective farms there were many examples of stealing and embezzlement. In construction there were billions of rubles unaccounted for from capital investment. Especially disappointing was the situation with accommodation, where the slowing in the construction of temporary accommodation was directly caused by diverting budget funds to prestigious socio-cultural monuments and tacky suburban housing for officials. These few apartments, built so poorly, were often abandoned to degradation and misuse.

Nazarbayev's efforts to open the informal discussion of such sore topics was met with misunderstanding, undisguised annoyance, and in some circles outright hostility. In his view, their intransigence only exacerbated the situation, demanding immediate and decisive action. However, given the backward-looking narrow-minded views prevailing, the only means to stir society into action remaining was through open discussion.

Dinmukhamed Kunayev and Nursultan Nazarbayev at one of the production centres.

In the February 1986 Sixteenth Congress of the Communist Party of Kazakhstan, in contrast to the usual watered-down reports and traditional rhetoric, a sharp point-by-point critique of all these negative attitudes came forth from the mouth of the Chairman of the Council of Ministers, Nursultan Nazarbayev. He was in no mood to be gainsaid. In the ensuing report the name of the leader of the republic was not once alluded to. But the basic message was directed to him.

An immediate response was demanded, and the apprehension of the 'dissidents' was urgently organized. Special agents were tasked with monitoring Nazarbayev's finances and to investigate as to whether he abused his official position and exploited government channels to satisfy his personal needs and out-of-office pursuits. But digging up dirty information proved fruitless.

Two years later a similar attack on Nazarbayev initiated from Gennady Kolbin, having replaced Kunaev in the post of First Secretary. Unable to scare, discredit, or dislodge Nazarbayev from his role through legitimate means, Kolbin resorted to the tried and tested tactic, using his connections to the Central Committee of the CPSU and the KGB of the USSR, which however also awaited catastrophe. In August 1989, in an interview in the newspaper *Izvestia*, Nazarbayev would say: 'After the Party congress of the republic, I exposed serious shortcomings in

attitudes and methods present in the leadership of the republic. That period of inertia was a hard time for me to live through. But for many a month I held firm. Moreover, it was an experience I had known before, on account of my unswerving independence of mind.'

A conflict between Nazarbayev and Kunaev seemed to be a classic example of intergenerational disagreement, as of fathers and sons. One faced towards the past, the other the future. Nazarbayev was acting in the name of a new generation of political leaders who were not prepared to accept Kazakhstan's role as 'a sanctuary of stagnation' and a second-grade food-providing republic.

All in all, 1986 was considered by Nazarbayev and the whole of the Kazakh nation as a dramatic experience.

On 16 December, at the plenary session of the Central Committee of Kazakhstan, Kunayev was relieved of his role of First Secretary. In his place Gennady Kolbin was appointed; he had worked until then as the First Secretary of Ulyanovsk regional CPSU and had had no connection with Kazakhstan.

With Perestroika's false start, the word was already discredited as a slogan. Indeed it had come to mean the opposite of what was intended. Kazakhs expressed themselves through the voices of those best entitled to represent them, who did not hold with the anticipated moves and the prospect of another lost period dubbed 'the second [19]37'.

The historic meeting of the Communist Party of Kazakhstan took place in February 1986 at what is today the impressive City Hall in Almaty. It was the 1986 site of the birth of the free Kazakhstan.

On 17 December, the young people, displeased by the endorsement by the Politburo of the Central Committee of the CPSU of the appointment of a new Secretary of the Communist Party of Kazakhstan, issued forth into the main square of Alma-Ata, then the capital of the republic, for a peaceful demonstration. The slogans were 'up with Lenin's national policy!', 'Each nation has the right to choose its own leader!', 'That's enough decrees!', 'Perestroika's happening, where's democracy?' The protesters proposed a re-run of the vote for First Minister of the Central Committee of the Communist Party of Kazakhstan, to be chosen from a raft of candidates familiar with local realities and based on intelligible policies and without regard for ethnicity.

The peaceful demonstration, albeit peaceful, was violently suppressed. Similar events were happening in Dzhezkazgan, Karaganda, Taldy-Kurgan, Arkalyk, Kokshetau, Pavlodar, Shymkent, Talgar and Saryozek – ten regional entities in all. Legal proceedings were then brought against the participants. Many were condemned, and a number of death penalties were dealt out.

Behind the response to that December's events were shallow values, the protests were dubbed 'the poets' revolt' or 'the nationalists' plot'. In reality, these events were the consequence of many socio-political stresses, uniting up over decades, such as the catastrophic decrease in the amount of national schools; marginalization of the national language, traditional religion and Kazakh culture; unrest amongst the youth; and a shortage of essential foodstuffs and consumer products. An extremely negative reaction was expected from the incapable and short-sighted central government. The sending in of an outsider as new secretary of the republic only seemed to pour oil on the flames. Then came the moment when all the frustrations and bitter resentments boiled over.

Such was the meaning of December's events. There followed unrest in Sumgait (in Azerbaijan), Tbilsi, Baku and Vilnius. It all went far beyond the USSR's inner-republic framework, opening the crisis onto the entire Soviet socialist system.

At the very beginning of the protest, Central Committee Party members met up on Young Peoples' Square to make their demands to the government. Moscow's stance was not to pay serious attention to the grievances and demands of the protesters. It ignored their attempt to find a compromise. Efforts to open a dialogue came to nothing. Moscow's people reserved the decision-making for themselves, and froze out local government from partaking in running the republic.

Nazarbayev recalls the situation: 'From the arrival from Moscow of representatives who categorically forbade us from intervening in what was happening in the square we were uncertain as to whether we could use the popular mood to achieve some of our aims. Some were scared by other demonstrators' demands to review the vote for the post of First Secretary. Among the candidates were E.N. Aulbekov, S.M. Mukasheva and Nazarbayev. Other names were put forward: V.P. Demidenko, O.S. Miroshhina, N.E. Morozov and more. Speaking for people in general, our own names as occurring in these documents bear witness to the protesters not just opposing a leader being of another nationality, but insisting he had to be a Kazakh. In the longer term, the decision was to redefine 'Kazakh nationality', which agitated the whole country. In those days Moscow officials only spoke to me with words of mistrust and alienation, always in an insulting and patronizing tone. In deciding on who would take the post of First Secretary, senior officials of the Party did not count the opinions of local constituencies, proving that candidates for this post were not assessed on any personal basis and were not even discussed amongst members of the Central Committee nor of the Bureau of the Central Committee.'

A wave of political repression flooded the republic. In July 1987, the Central Committee of the CPSU issued the decree 'Concerning the Work of the Kazakh Republic Party Organization in the International and Political Education of Workers' – essentially accusing the entire Kazakh nation of nationalism.

With the exit of Kolbin in the spring of 1989, among the prime duties in the post of First Secretary for Nursultan Nazarbayev was to revive fairness and secure a change to this decree. He constantly posed questions on the issue to the Politburo and the head of the Soviet government, Mikhail Gorbachev, regarding the role of the Kazakh nation and the accusation of nationalism. Hence the fiery defence of the honour of his homeland in the Plenary Meeting of the Central Committee of the CPSU in Moscow from 19–20 September 1989.

Nazarbayev drew together his arguments. 'The decree released was not only unfair, but insulting to the nation's inhabitants. For example, it created an impression of Kazakh "nationalism". But in principle, can this nation be entirely to blame for such anti-human characterization? I'm deeply convinced that No, it cannot. Speaking on behalf of the opinions of all Communists, I request that the Central Committee

Alma-Ata, L.I. Brezhnev Square, December 1986.

reviews these mistaken official positions, and addresses the injury to the honour and decency of the Kazakh nation, which has cast a shadow on its international presence.'

As a result, a special decree was released by the Politburo on 18 May 1990 'Regarding the Work of the Kazakh Republic Party Organization for the International and Political Education of Workers'. It was published in *Publication No. 6, Proceedings of the CC CPSU*, in which the second point spoke of 'the acknowledgement that in the decree on the evaluation of the masses, the accusation of violating social order in the town of Alma-Ata in December 1986 as a sign of Kazakh nationalism is a mistake.' Thus, as a result of the insistent demands and actions of Nazarbayev, state participation in the multinational Kazakh society was strengthened, and the slanderous decree retracted. There followed reviews of many of the unlawfully convicted 'Decembrists' who were quickly freed from imprisonment and absolved of guilt.

Simultaneously, Nazarbayev was taking measures to stabilize the situation in the republic. In his speeches, he constantly drew attention to the value of the December events and spoke about the need to withhold publication of unproven witness accounts and led to unnecessary agitation. It was not allowed, he noted, for the national pride of one nation to be asserted at the expense of the esteem of another. He expressed a call: not to dwell in the past and live by old prejudices, but consolidate the strengths already there in society for the sake of a decent future.

One of the most succinct political evaluations arising from the December events of 1986 was to be found in the words of Nazarbayev spoken on 5 September 1992 at a meeting of the Kazakh and Kyrgyzstan youth in the Zhambyl area of the Alma-Ata region. 'These events were the start of a new epoch. Zheltoksan was not an act by one nation against another, but became the first expression of protest from millions of people striving for freedom against the menace of a totalitarian system. Across the whole former Union, these events were the first democratic breakthrough by a nation in motion. Our young boys and girls were the first carriers of a wind of change, bringing a long awaited freedom not only to Kazakhstan, but to many nations of Europe and Asia. They had, by the naked hand, to defend the tender plants of a progressive democracy. Yes, it will be remembered in centuries, the heroic spirit of the Kazakh youth!'

In 2006, on the twentieth anniversary of the Decembrist event, the solemn opening of the memorial 'the light of independence' was to take place in the centre of Almaty. Speaking at that occasion Nazarbayev said: 'Twenty years ago our youth gathered here, in order to express its decisive protest against the tyrannical and disingenuous politics of the totalitarian system – which had argued that "Kazakhs are not suited for self determination; among them were none born a leader" – such as to direct their nation with their own leader, not relegated by our history, culture, language and religion. The strength of these young people was acknowledged at the time in Gorbachev's announcement in 1985 of Glasnost and democratization, in which they expressed their disagreement. This was not only a sign of bravery but of mature citizenship. All of us know that the initially peaceful non-violent attitude towards democratization of the youth was to end. They rejected the abuse and victimization that would follow – the violation of rights, the harsh repression – today, mere history. It is necessary not to dwell on the past for the sake of moving forward ... This memorial, on one hand, is for those who suffered and for the blood poured from those who opposed the totalitarian system; and on the other a symbol of our bright future.'

5

Time for Action

On the 22 June 1989 Nursultan Nazarbayev was voted First Secretary of the Communist Party of Kazakhstan's Central Committee. As the ensuing eventful and turbulent times demonstrated, the day marked a turning point in the history of Kazakhstan.

V.M. Chebrikov had flown in from Moscow for the Fifteenth Plenary Session of the Central Committee of the Communist Party of Kazakhstan. He belonged to the Politburo of the Communist Party of the Soviet Union. 'The Politburo', he declared 'discussed the candidates for the role of First Secretary of the Central Committee at great length. The decision was made to recommend to you, the Plenary Session, that you elect comrade Nazarbayev to the role. There is no need for me to recite the biography of the chosen candidate; you will all know him from your work together. Nursultan Nazarbayev completed his education here, in the Republic; he knows precisely what has been done, and what needs to be done to further the work of Perestroika in the Republic. I call upon you to support the Politburo's recommendation to elect comrade Nursultan Nazarbayev as First Secretary of the Communist Party of Kazakhstan.'

Amid the industrial grass roots, Nazarbayev (centre) brings to his leadership endurance and prudence.

Opposite and above:
Nazarbayev, as First Secretary, defends the interests of the emerging free Republic.

Many speakers at the Plenary Session spoke of Nazarbayev as 'one of the main architects of Perestroika in Kazakhstan' and concluded in their speeches that Nazarbayev, thanks to his life experience and the toughening in the worlds of work and politics, had become a true leader. A particular impression was left by the words of S.V. Drozhin, a veteran of the metallurgical industry. 'I have known Nursultan Abishuly for eighteen years,' he said. 'In these difficult years of growth for the Karaganda Metallurgical Plant he worked as Secretary of the Party Committee. I am a working man, and he is a party official but there have never been any barriers between us. The Secretary's office was always open to everyone, although his place of work was often more like the busy shop floor of the plant than an office. I can tell you simply that you can work well with a man like this.'

After debating Nazarbayev's candidature the Central Committee held its first ever secret ballot in which 158 members of the Committee took part – 154 voted for and 4 against. The result of the ballot was upheld and Nazarbayev was duly elected First Secretary.

The last speaker of the Plenary Session was Nazarbayev himself. 'I understand the full weight of responsibility placed upon both the Central Committee and upon myself directly in this difficult and pivotal moment in the history of our country. All Soviet people think of Perestroika as the solution to important socio-economic and political problems. This includes international relations, which in quieter times has slipped into the background. We must now intensify our attention to this question. My position in this regard is well known. It was laid out in my speech to the First Assembly of the National Delegates of the Soviet Union. I would like to assure you all that I will do my utmost to put this theory into practice.'

Nazarbayev's role as Party Secretary began under most unfavourable conditions; this was a momentous turning point for Kazakhstan, and the fate of the Kazakh people and the Republic itself hung in the balance. The nascent Perestroika programme was not fulfilling its expectations – either to reinvigorate the economy or to improve people's standard of living.

Towards the end of the 1980s the economic outlook darkened drastically. Meanwhile disagreements between the Soviet Union and its republics, worsening inter-ethnic relations and social strife, and ongoing ideological divisions in the Communist Party of the Soviet Union were leading to a host of complex problems.

In Kazakhstan, as with the whole of the Soviet Union, 'protest democracy' became the order of the day. The people's discontent flared up into spontaneous demonstrations, like those in Zhanaozen (also known as Novy Uzen), and strikes in the region's major industrial plants. On top of this were ominous outbreaks of civil and inter-ethnic conflict in the South Caucasus, Uzbekistan, Transnistria and the Baltic states.

Faced with this situation Nazarbayev had to concentrate on the most pressing issues: a programme of radical economic reform, clear separation of governmental powers, and strengthening of inter-ethnic relations and social stability.

He highlighted the problems facing Kazakhstan, along with his vision for solving them, at the First Assembly of the National Delegates of the Soviet Union. In his focused address he detailed twelve interconnected issues, each requiring urgent attention.

1. Reduction of the trade deficit and inflation both of which were undermining the prosperity of all citizens.
2. The economic imbalance where, despite economic growth, the production of consumer goods had shrunk below demand.

A television address to the people of Kazakhstan given by the new President in the late 1980s.

3. Refining the model of Khozraschyot (introducing the profit motive to Soviet economics), which was devised without regard for local requirements.

4. Termination of unilateral activities on the part of councils and ministries and an end to the monopoly enjoyed by the USSR's arms industry.

5. Rectifying the ecological catastrophes in Semipalatinsk and the Aral Sea caused by the testing of biological weapons and other polluting activities.

6. Removing inequality from the distribution of profits between the central budget and the budget of the republics.

7. An end to discrimination on the part of the central authorities which denies local people access to shared strategic sites (such as Baikonur Space Launch Facility, Maikain etc).

8. Greater autonomy for local executive branches of government.

9. Reducing civil unrest and reaffirming the need for discipline both in industry and in society in general.

10. Fostering good international relations, and not confusing the crimes of totalitarianism with the character of the Russian people, who had suffered under it more than most.

11. Increased representation for the republics on a state level.

12. Denunciation of all attacks against the good name of the Kazakh people, unfairly and crudely labelled nationalists since the events of December 1986.

To make such an address in Moscow in front of the leadership of what remained the almighty centre of power of the Soviet Union took exceptional courage.

Nazarbayev used his platform as a national deputy of the USSR (1989–91), to promote with skill and passion the interests of the Republic. In fact, through the initiative of a group of delegates both from central government and from various autonomous republics Nazarbayev was put forward at the very same meeting for the role of

The new Republic, the President urges, must bring results.

vice-president of the USSR. This was not an isolated event. Two years later, in 1991, he was nominated for the role of Chairman of the Cabinet of the USSR.

A sharp fall in the economy and the collapse of inter-regional trade relationships coupled with ongoing mismanagement in industry led to a growing chaos, which the central authority's incoherent actions could not prevent. This crisis threatened to worsen the trade and food deficits and to plunge the whole population into hardship.

As the crisis deepened Nazarbayev took measures to achieve stability; he directed the focus of the country's economy towards natural resources, strengthened internal trade within the Republic, and established a united internal economic zone.

However, political control remained with the central authorities, and they were unwilling, sometimes against all common sense, to cede power to the Soviet republics. Hence all attempts at economic reform were doomed, if not to failure, then to long delays. This led to acrimony in the discussions of the Union Accord.

Nursultan Nazarbayev was one of the key ideologues promoting a devolution of power to the republics, often stressing that completing the Union Accord quickly was not necessarily the main point. Many ecological disasters of the time, such as the Aral Sea and the Semipalatinsk Test Site, were attributable to the central Soviet authorities. The main reasons were a lack of accountability and criminality among central ministries with direct control over 90 per cent of Kazakhstan industry.

Nazarbayev met strong resistance from the Soviet bureaucracy, in particular the leaders of the Industry and Defence Committee. However, as a pragmatic leader he fully understood that there was no other option available.

In 1990, the repeated failure on the part of the central authorities to move forward with the Union Accord continued. Nazarbayev set to work developing the project from within Kazakhstan. The key ideas he was putting forward were the same as those already presented to the people of Kazakhstan in his speech 'For Unity and Consolidation', given via television on the 10 September 1990. 'We are starting to formulate a whole new political premise – a union of sovereign states. The motivation is clear: the republics will gain an unprecedented level of control over their own national wealth. This includes the land, natural resources, water, airspace and other natural assets, as well as the scientific and technical potential which together form the material basis of a state's sovereignty. The Union itself is based on the principle of voluntary participation, shared interests and an equal footing for each republic.

'It stands to reason that the republics will delegate a part of their power to specially formulated administrative bodies which will be in charge of activities requiring organization on a statewide scale. These include essential research, defence, the energy network, nuclear power, the space programme and similar activities.'

Nazarbayev's principled position on economic and political reform of the USSR met with support not just from politicians but the general public. It is no surprise that at this time he joined the ranks of the USSR's most authoritative and influential politicians and gained wide popular support.

Using his newly found political influence, he turned his attention to his country's ecological problems, principally the Aral Sea catastrophe, the fallout from the Semipalatinsk Test Site, a scarcity of fresh water and industrial pollution.

The most pressing of these issues was the Aral Sea and the rehabilitation of the region surrounding it. Nazarbayev did not approach this problem simply from a socio-economic standpoint but rather placed emphasis on the historical importance of the Aral Region and the Syr Darya Valley which formed the ancestral heartland of the people of Central Asia and was the site of over forty highly economically and culturally advanced cities.

The Aral Sea and Syr Darya River began to dry up in the second half of the twentieth century due to an extravagant expansion of cotton and rice growing with all of the irrigation systems, canals and reservoirs. All this had plunged the region between the Amu Darya and the Syr Darya into ecological disaster.

By the end of the twentieth century the Aral Sea had lost three quarters of its water. All that remained were two separate lakes, the North Aral Sea and the South Aral Sea, both within the territory of Kazakhstan, which together covered an area of just 60,000 square kilometres. A separate system of some 3000 small lakes around the sea's perimeter had been reduced to salt marshes. Besides the salt and minerals that polluted the Syr Darya basin the area was further blighted by chemical effluent from the fertilizers of the surrounding rice and cotton fields. What was once impenetrable forest and riparian woodland was now sand and claypan, and a former plethora of fauna had been brought to the point of extinction. All of this turned what was once a

Aral – pain and hope.

balanced and hospitable climate into a place where the summer days can reach a humid 45 degrees, and in winter months the temperature regularly falls below 40.

The river water, which for centuries had been used for drinking, had become unfit not just for human consumption but for animals too. According to research by medical scientists the level of sulphites in the early 2000s was fifteen times higher than average, of nitrates five times higher and of magnesium three to four times. These pollutants have had a malign impact on residents of the area.

A genuine effort to rehabilitate the Aral Sea only began with Kazakhstan gaining independence. In an attempt to bring the problem of the Aral Sea to the world's attention, Nazarbayev raised the question

in October 1992 at the forty-seventh Session of the UN General Assembly.

Thanks to his initiative in 1993 an international fund was established to help save the region. This involved the cooperation of Uzbekistan and Turkmenistan with the Kazakh government.

At the same time the huge international project entitled Regulation of the Syr Darya Watercourse and Saving of the Northern Part of the Aral Sea began to take shape, thanks to financial support from the International Bank for Reconstruction and Development. Around the start of the 2000s a national project with the same aims was also created.

As part of these projects the watercourse of the Syr Darya River was cleared to improve water flow and a dyke was built (called Dike Kokaral) between the larger South Aral Sea and the smaller North Aral Sea. The purpose of the dyke was to raise the water level of the North Aral Sea and so reduce the salinity of the water level to increase marine life.

The outcome of this will be to bring life back to an area marred sand, salt and blizzards. The ecology of the whole region will become progressively healthier; the economy will strengthen. Eventually the

The President's message is one of 'unity in diversity'.

people of the Aral Region will return to their traditional land. The attempt to bring life back to the Aral Region has already been dubbed by some western experts as a 'Biblical miracle'.

Another issue receiving Nazarbayev's attention was interethnic relations within the state. The end of the 1980s was marked by an explosion in the level of self-awareness among all of the different ethnic groups of the USSR. After decades of censorship people began to speak openly about the casualties of economic growth; the homogenization of culture across the USSR, the loss of national character, customs and traditions, and the threat of extinction that loomed over many native languages.

In Kazakhstan this process took place within a complex moral and psychological climate because of the events of December 1986 (the Zheltoksan Riots). The issue of identity amongst the country's many ethnicities carried with it the painful legacy of punitive repression.

As the saying goes: 'A spark left unextinguished becomes a flame, an illness left uncured becomes suffering.' It was clear that a successful transition to an integrated multiethnic republic was not possible without trust first being restored between its ethnic compatriots.

The first signs of a somewhat bitter discord arose over the new law on language. Nazarbayev took an active role in the formation of the new law and brought to bear a balanced and subtle understanding of the problem. He took a centrist approach and was able to give equal representation to all of the languages without favouring any unduly. Before the parliamentary debates had even begun Nazarbayev gave a speech 'On the Organizational and Political Work of Party Members Towards Promoting Perestroika' and took the opportunity to announce the new law. He said, 'Very soon a new law will be announced relating to languages within Kazakhstan. A large group of scholars and cultural specialists have been working on this law for a long time. It is not my role to give an exhaustive evaluation of this document. The law will be tested against the judgement of each and every Kazakh citizen. I will say only this: the proper conception of this law differs from that of analogous laws in other republics. They were passed solely to strengthen their own international presence. The criterion informing the creation of this law was the basic thought that true prosperity for a nation cannot be achieved at the cost of a derogation of the rights and freedom of constituent nationalities. An inclusive community recognizes that the way to effectively protect a language lying at the heart of its nation is to endow it with government status. The same legal channels will then be open to the languages of all other nationalities, providing them the same opportunities for growth. In this way Russian, as a language of international communication, will rightfully keep its role, but beyond it will lie a space for the rigorous intellectual potential of each nationality, and each person.' Thanks to this tactful approach the law was passed in Kazakhstan in September 1989. Some of the animosity was taken out of interethnic relations, bringing a newly found stability to the Republic.

Nazarbayev was convinced that lasting development of Kazakhstan could only occur alongside the cultural development of all of its ethnic groups. In order to meet this aim a series of cultural centres were opened in 1989. It culminated in 1995 with the opening of the Assembly of the People of Kazakhstan. Many people began to renew ties to their past which had long since been severed. This included many descendants of exiled Germans, Koreans, Poles, Lithuanians, Crimean Tatars, Meskhetian Turks, Vainakhs, Karachays, Balkars, Greeks and others.

In order to reunite the historic Kazakh people including those of the global diaspora an organization was formed in 1992 with Nazarbayev as its head. The organization acts as a cultural hearth for the Kazakh race and is called the World Association of Kazakhs.

Nazarbayev also became the first Soviet leader of Kazakhstan to reject the traditional anti-religious ideology of Communism and began to re-involve religious institutions in cultural life. On 25 September 1989 he met with a large group of religious leaders including the Muslim Qadi of Kazakhstan, R. Nysanbayev, the head of the Alma-Ata and Kazakhstan dioceses of the Russian Orthodox Church, Bishop Yevseviy, the elder of the Council of Evangelical Baptists of Kazakhstan, Gorelov, and the elder preacher of the Kazakhstan Church of the Seventh-day Adventists, Vel'gosha, among others. The session was successful and he resolved to repeat the meetings regularly.

Nazarbayev's open and tolerant approach to religion was met with much gratitude and support from those who had undergone decades of persecution and had been forced into hiding at the hands of the USSR's militant atheism and religious suppression.

The meeting of September 1989 was one of the first steps towards a new policy of religious tolerance and cooperation which was to become a hallmark of Kazakh society and would find its expression in constitutional guarantees of pluralism, tolerance, and religious freedom, inspiring the renovation of old churches and the building of new ones. The historic visit of Pope John Paul II in 2001 further cemented

Kazakhstan's new role as a global beacon of religious and interfaith dialogue.

Given the confused and contradictory policy of the central authorities, Nazarbayev's own honest economic mistakes and other obstacles to the progress of the Union Accord, Nazarbayev was forced to take a series of preventative measures to protect the interests of the Republic and safeguard its independence.

As the movement towards devolution gained momentum the need to consolidate power at the level of the republics grew. Towards this end Nazarbayev was chosen for the post of Chairman of the Supreme Council of the Communist Party of Kazakhstan. His power was cemented on 24 April of the same year with his appointment by the Supreme Council to the role of President of the Communist Party of Kazakhstan. The experience of the previous few years had shown that strengthening the role of the President was important and would have a decisive influence on the shape of the emerging independent government, as well as providing assurances of the state's survival after the collapse of the Soviet Union.

6

On the Brink of Independence

One of Nazarbayev's first actions as President was to establish an institutional structure for Kazakhstan's imminent political and economic sovereignty.

The inauguration of Kazakhstan's first President came at a time of deep crisis within the USSR which had reached all corners of the government and society at large. The economy in particular was failing badly. The shattering of long-standing business practices of the former economic system led to a sharp drop in standards of living and to social instability in general.

As the economic situation worsened, so did interethnic tensions across the whole Soviet Union. In the face of these problems the once mighty Communist Party was powerless, suffering a severe lack of resources.

The emblem of Kazakhstan's ancient right to independence – the Golden Man.

In light of this state of affairs Nazarbayev was keen to distance himself from the Communist Party, taking the opportunity to consolidate Kazakhstan's independence.

His first step was the 'Declaration of Sovereignty of the State of Kazakhstan' made on 25 October 1990 by the Supreme Council under the President. This law became the founding legislative act of the nascent state, and guaranteed the country's further development into a completely independent state. Moreover, it underlined Kazakhstan's principle dividing state powers into legislative, executive and judicial branches. It was decided that legislative powers would be given to the Supreme Council, judicial powers to the High Court, and that the executive powers to the Head of State, President Nazarbayev.

In order to bring about political and economic change, as well as to defend the independence of the new Republic, it was necessary to restructure all of the state's political systems and to redistribute power accordingly. To this end, on 20 November 1990, the President passed a new law 'On the Rationalization of Kazakhstan's Political Power Structures and the Introduction of Amendments to the Constitution'. In accordance with the law the roles of vice-president, prime minister and other government ministers were created, and the Council of Ministers and Cabinet of Ministers were founded. The Council of the Republic was also created as a consultative board for the President.

Local and regional councils were also reorganized under the new law; their powers were extended and they were given greater control over their role in the market economy and over industries in their respective regions.

The reforms were not always popular, and the President met with immediate resistance from several different directions. The CPSU was particularly opposed to the proposals, made between April 1990 and August 1991, and a bitter power battle between the Kazakh Communist Party and the President took place.

Political change, of course, particularly upset those with something to lose: Party and council members and industry officials of middle age or older who had managed to appropriate some level of political capital, and who had career prospects and a leisurely retirement awaiting them. 'Don't change anything,' they said, 'Let us live out the end of this century in peace, then you can do what you want!' Unfortunately this attitude was commonplace and the people who supported it formed a significant and influential portion of society.

Kazakhstan's Declaration of Sovereignty.

Nazarbayev, President of the Soviet Republic of Kazakhstan, meets industry pioneers. Alma-Ata, 1990.

Another unexpected ideological rival to the President was the Supreme Council. Having gained a new lease of life from Perestroika (under the slogan 'all the power of the Council') the members of the Supreme Council should have been staunch allies of the President. However, because of their allegiance to the system of one-party rule the Council was vehemently opposed to this form of presidential power and democratic reforms in general.

In response to growing opposition from the Soviet Union, Nazarbayev broached this issue on 20 December 1990 at the Fourth Congress of the Regional Delegates of the USSR. He said 'In recent times there has been much criticism of the so-called "sovereign bandwagon", but those who do so are sorely mistaken if they see only parochialism and selfish ambition in the new sovereign states. The real motivations for change are the total paralysis and egoism of the central authorities and their refusal to give up their dictatorship. Their greed has brought about economic collapse, a loss of law and order and interethnic conflict. Will you throw stones at those republics which seek, one way or another, to escape political collapse? Will you accuse them of separatism simply because they display a healthy desire for self-preservation among growing chaos?'

At the same meeting Nazarbayev launched an attack on the President of the Soviet Union, Mikhail Gorbachev, claiming that his inconsistency and incompetence made him unable to carry through the reforms he himself had planned.

The final days of a superpower at the Kremlin, Moscow.

Meanwhile, the situation in the Soviet Union grew steadily worse. Nazarbayev, all too aware of the impending collapse of the Soviet Union, told Gorbachev that 'any attempt to grab power, especially using the army or the police force, will only provoke more violence and will not bring stability'.

Just a few months later, Nazarbayev was proved right.

From 19–21 August 1991 an attempted coup was made on the Soviet Union, now known as the August Putsch. The attempt was made by reactionary elements of the Central Communist Party State Committee on the State of Emergency, a group of eight high-level officials within the Soviet government. The eight members of the committee were the Vice-President of the USSR, G.I. Yanayev, the Prime Minister, V.S. Pavlov, the chief assistant to the Secretary of Defence, O.D. Baklanov, the Head of the KGB, B.A. Kryuchkov, the Defence Minister, D.T. Yazov, the Minister for Internal Affairs, B.K. Pugo, the President of the Association for State Industry, Transport, and Construction, A.I. Tizyakov, and the President of the Christian Union of the USSR, V.A. Starodubtsev.

Both Gorbachev's ejection from the presidency and the ensuing failure of the coup led to the signing of the 'Agreement of the Union of Sovereign States' on 20 August 1991.

In every person's life there are moments when his or her strength is tested. In such moments the weak stumble but the strong only emerge stronger, ready for what is to come. This is the true crossing of the Rubicon, where a person gains full knowledge of themselves.

Right and below:
Moscow, August 1991.

Only Nursultan Nazarbayev himself can truly understand what he went through in this period, bearing responsibility for himself, his nation and its history on his shoulders.

From the very start the actions of the State Committee were highly provocative. V.A. Kryuchkov first contacted Nazarbayev by telephone, compelling him to submit to the Committee. Later he was told by G.I. Yanayev, his supposed second in command, that all of the other Soviet republics had already acquiesced, a lie he repeated afterwards at a press conference. One lie may be forgiven, but on 21 August the Committee went so far as to attempt to deploy troops in the capital of Kyrgyzstan. In short, the August Putsch came within a hair's breadth of causing civil war.

A contemporaneous chronological account of Nazarbayev's actions has survived in a diary he kept between 19 and 21 August 1991. In its

Left, below and opposite:
Album pictures.

tense, narrow lines it is impossible not to feel the pain and anxiety that he felt for the fate of the country and his desire and determination to do everything he could to protect it. They vividly convey the electric atmosphere of the time, where the situation could explode at any moment.

On 19 August at 2pm the President wrote the following note: 'Joint meeting of the SC Presidium [Supreme Council] and the CM [Cabinet of Ministers]. Overview. Discussion. Text of the address corresponds [dissuaded]. Said that I will be held responsible.'

On the same day, Nazarbayev made a radio announcement in which he reassured the people of Kazakhstan that he would maintain the peace and rebuff any extremist provocation. He also reaffirmed his unswerving commitment to independence and democracy. This speech turned out to be very timely and played an important role in maintaining stability in the country, reassuring society that their nation was in safe hands.

Directly after this address the President began to prepare a statement to the people of the USSR. This was not spontaneous; as an experienced politician he was all too aware that the fate of his country hung in the balance, and that a fine line lay between totalitarianism and freedom – the past and the future.

The statement, which directly criticized the organizers of the attempted coup, was transmitted on 20 August. At 7.30 that evening

the President wrote: 'My statement. Illegality of the State Committee on the State of Emergency. Transmitted by the republics. Central press won't transmit it, won't print it.'

At the same time Nazarbayev gave his official resignation from the CPSU.

Moreover, fearing that one of the world's greatest powers, the USSR, could descend into bloodshed, Nazarbayev took on the difficult job of intermediary between the Communist Party and the democratic movement headed by Boris Yeltsin. Countless telephone calls between himself and the Communist Party leaders, Yeltsin, and the leaders of the Soviet republics, A.A. Akayev and L.M. Kravchuk, attest to his

involvement. 'I was ready to go to Moscow at a moment's notice,' he later recalled. Despite being thousands of kilometres away, the President took a prominent role in the events of August 1991.

When news came of a gathering storm at the Supreme Council of the RSFSR, Nazarbayev was called to another meeting with Kryuchkov, Yanayev, Yazov and Yeltsin. The meeting continued through the nights of 20 and 21 August until the storm had been averted.

Below:
Moscow, August 1991: the Soviet Union collapses.

Above:
Album picture.

Above right:
Rallying support for the closure of Semipalatinsk nuclear test site.

'I heard about the trouble at the Supreme Council on the evening of 20 August,' recalled Nazarbayev. 'I was in contact with Kryuchkov. The former chairman of the Safety Committee assured me that there would be no problems at the Council. I knew that it would be better not to trust him so I spoke to Yeltsin several times on the telephone, the only one still working at the Council building, as it happened … Yeltsin confirmed the disturbing news. I told Boris that he had my complete support and then immediately rang Yanayev. I told him of my displeasure at what was happening and warned him how serious the consequences would be if a forcible attack were launched against the Supreme Council. Next I called Yazov, by which point it was the morning of 21 August. I said to him: "You are a soldier, you've experienced war. Don't let the blood of our children be on your hands. The youth are our future." I told him to get the military out of there. Maybe it had an impact.'

On the eve of the signing of the new Union Agreement, events surrounding the unconstitutional coup attempt revealed the unsuitability of the central authorities and their ideology of a single united government for the new era. They discredited the Communist Party and hastened the collapse of the USSR, drawing the era of Soviet superpower to a close.

On 29 August 1991, shortly after the failure of the coup, Nazarbayev signed an order for the 'closing of the Semipalatinsk nuclear test site', marking an irrevocable step towards independence.

Events at the Semipalatinsk test site, starting in mid 1989 and lasting until its eventual closure, showed cooperation between the leadership of Kazakhstan and the grassroots group 'Nevada-Semipalatinsk', led by the famous poet and public figure Olzhas Suleimenov. This was one of the first examples of effective cooperation between the state and the new civil society.

It is no secret that the collapse of the Soviet Union left Kazakhstan with the fourth largest nuclear arsenal in the world (after the USA, Russia and the Ukraine) comprising 104 SS-18 intercontinental ballistic missiles, nicknamed 'Satan' in the West, and a strategic base, with 1400 warheads and forty Tu-95 MS bomber aircraft with 240 cruise missiles. Because of the arms race between the USSR and the USA, Kazakhstan's arsenal was bigger than that of Great Britain, France and China combined.

Moreover, Kazakhstan was not just a nuclear weapons storage and launching site. Following the collapse of the USSR the country inherited the infrastructure needed for the modernization and manufacture of nuclear weapons. Beginning in 1949, a total of 468 nuclear explosions were carried out at a variety of test sites across the Republic. Out of these tests ninety-one were conducted above the ground, twenty-six at ground level, eight at high altitude and 343 below ground. The power of the warheads ranged from several kilotons to 1.5 megatons, and when combined the power of these bombs was 2500 times greater than that of the bomb dropped on Hiroshima in 1945.

Activists from the international nuclear disarmament campaign Nevada-Semipalatinsk.

The decree declaring the end of the Semipalatinsk nuclear test site, October 1989.

The President meets the first two astronauts of independent Kazakhstan: Toktar Aubakirov and Talgat Musabayev.

Thus, the question of the legacy of the Soviet nuclear arsenal arose; if not the single most important issue of the day, it was recognized as one which would affect the whole country. As Head of State, responsibility fell on Nazarbayev. During a time of crisis he had to decide whether Kazakhstan should remain a nuclear power.

The protection afforded by the country's nuclear weapons was considered an important guarantee of its sovereignty. Nazarbayev fully understood this position, yet also understood the great dangers that came with nuclear weapons.

Despite the fact that the President's desire had long been for complete nuclear disarmament, the country's national security required a different position: Kazakhstan would not dismantle its nuclear arsenal without a guarantee of its safety from the world's nuclear powers, in particular from members of the 'Nuclear Club'. Nazarbayev made it clear to the world that he would only be willing to alter Kazakhstan's nuclear status if the conditions were mutually favourable. In order to cement the deal Kazakhstan would seek a promise of support for its program of modernization.

The negotiation process was arduous but in the end Kazakh diplomacy won the day, and Nazarbayev's position was upheld. Representatives from the nuclear states, including the USA, Russia, Great Britain, France and China gave Kazakhstan a firm guarantee that they would protect both its safety and sovereignty over its territory.

Kazakhstan also received essential economic help from several key international organizations including the World Bank and the International Monetary Fund.

In the following five years, with the participation of the USA and Russia, Kazakhstan revealed the full extent of its arsenal. The state also signed the Treaty on the Non-Proliferation of Nuclear Weapons and the Comprehensive Nuclear-Test-Ban Treaty and became a leader of the worldwide campaign for nuclear disarmament. Nazarbayev would later give a detailed account of these events in his book, *Epicentre of Peace.*

Another important step on the path to independence, following shortly after the closing of the Semipalatinsk Test Site, was the flight of

Top and above left:
The young President goes out to greet the voters on the eve of Kazakhstan's independence, 1991.

Above:
Boris Yeltsin presides over the Commonwealth of wholly independent ex-Soviet republics in Alma-Ata, 1991.

Kazakhstan's first cosmonaut, Toktar Aubakirov, on 2 October 1991. Nazarbayev played an important role in this remarkable event. He wholeheartedly wanted the project to be successful and guided it every step of the way. Despite countless discussions with the heads of various astronautic and military agencies, a meeting with Gorbachev was required to bring the project to fruition.

Several years later Nazarbayev once again took an active role in the Kazakh space programme when Talgat Musabayev became the first Kazakh citizen to go into space. Musabayev gave homage to the President in a brief statement: 'If it weren't for the President there would be no Kazakh astronauts.'

Following these events the first national presidential election was held on 1 December 1991. Across the twenty-one constituencies of Kazakhstan there were a total of 9,961,242 citizens of which 88.23 per cent (8,788,726 people) turned out to vote. The electoral bulletin named Nazarbayev as a candidate for President of Kazakhstan and E.M. Asanbayev as a candidate for Vice-President. The election resulted in 8,681,276 votes for Nazarbayev – a majority of 98.78 per cent.

Nazarbayev was inaugurated as President of the Republic of Kazakhstan on 10 December 1991.

The ceremony was attended by delegates from the USSR, members of the Council of Republics, heads of various ministries and government bodies, the chairs of regional and municipal councils, members of the Communist Party of Kazakhstan, members of the Central Electoral Commission, public figures in the fields of science, culture and art, the heads of political parties and civic societies, members of the clergy and representatives of the press.

The opening speech was given by the Chair of the Supreme Council, S.A. Abdil'din. In it he said, 'For the first time in Kazakhstan's history we have elected a President. The honour of this title goes to the great son of the Kazakh people, Nursultan Abishuly Nazarbayev. In an open and democratic vote almost 99 per cent of those who came to the polling stations gave their voice in his support. This is stark confirmation of the popularity and authority of Nursultan Abishuly within every section of society.

'In these difficult times the Kazakh nation has placed its trust in Nazarbayev, and given him full reponsiblity for the revival of our sovereign republic. At this morning session of Parliament we would like to declare that our nation shall henceforth be known as the Republic of Kazakhstan.'

In accordance with the constitution Nazarbayev took the Presidential Oath of Allegiance and gave his inaugural speech. It consisted of a strategic outline of the key ideas that were to shape and revive our country and bring Kazakhstan to the world stage.

Emphasizing that 'not every generation gets to witness and take part in such profound historical change', Nazarbayev laid out a series of initial tasks that befell the new state. 'Politics', he said, 'is about the division of power; it's about the formation of structures which create simple and effective organization; it's about transforming the Supreme Council into a professional Parliament which involves all of our delegates and local councils; it's about maintaining political pluralism

The first President swearing allegiance at his date of office.

whilst excluding all forms of extremism and nationalism or other forms of separatism that threaten the integrity of the Republic; it's about the decisive defence of law and order; it's about maintaining interethnic relations and ensuring the rights of every Kazakh citizen; and it's about upholding political stability as the basic principle of government politics.

'Without these political principles as our basis we cannot bring Kazakhstan into the realms of modern civilization, nor can we bring about the economic reform that our country needs. We need these principles in order to bring about the planned release of price controls, privatization, the establishment of a market infrastructure and a fair system of property rights. We must do away with all bureaucratic barriers to the growth of public and private enterprise which will underpin our economic renaissance.

'We are all feeling the hardships of this transitional period – the increase in prices, inflation, the deficit and the drop in living standards. Life is not so easy at the moment. I cannot and will not promise that it will get better soon; it would be dishonest of me not to say as much. We must grit our teeth and place our hope in the future.'

The Declaration of the Commonwealth of Independent States, signed in Alma-Ata.

On 16 December the Supreme Council passed the constitutional law 'On the Independence of the Government of the Republic of Kazakhstan' which marked the beginning of our country's total independence. The document, developed by Nazarbayev, declared Kazakhstan's complete power over its territories and the right to manage its own national and foreign affairs. The territorial boundaries of the former Soviet state became those of the nascent Republic and the territory was declared indivisible and inviolable. Citizens of every nationality were brought together into a single united Kazakh people and were granted the power to choose their own political representation.

The emergence of the Commonwealth of Independent States (CIS) onto the world map was a dramatic event. It was officially founded by the signing of a mutual agreement on 8 December 1991 in the Białowieza Forest. The document was signed by the Russian President Yeltsin, the Belorussian President S.S. Shushkevich and the Ukrainian President Kravchuk. The republics of Central Asia and the South Caucasus saw the formation of the CIS as an attempt to unify the Slavic nations and so their reaction was guarded. In response the leaders of five Central Asian governments met on 13 December in Ashgabat, the capital of Turkmenistan, to discuss the possibility of forming an organization of Central Asian states that would be a counterpoint to the nascent CIS. In the end it was only Nazarbayev's authoritativeness, along with his ability to convince the other states to join the newly formed Commonwealth, that prevented a new geopolitical hostility.

Thus Nazarbayev gained long-awaited independence for his native Kazakhstan, and began a new era in the Republic's long history.

7

Keeping Faith in Tomorrow

Kazakhstan's first years of independence at the beginning were, from a political perspective, its tensest and most crucial; the totalitarian system was dismantled, a market economy was established, and the complex search for a new model of government began. It was an important and dramatic period in which a new country was being born, as the foundations of its state were laid and it slowly started to be recognized by the international community. It was also in these years that the political and judicial framework of modern Kazakhstan began to appear, as key reforms led the transition from the Communist system towards one of democratic freedoms and economic diversity. It is a wonder that the country did not burst from the pressure of this upheaval, with changes of unprecedented scale following one another at lightning speed.

The President at work for national unity.

Left, above and opposite:
Nazarbayev urges the Supreme
Council to back the speeding
of reform.

Kazakhstan was being transformed from a totalitarian Communist system to a modern free-market society. And, unlike the Baltic States and other states of the former Soviet Bloc, for whom post-totalitarian transition meant a return to the liberal-bourgeois traditions of old, Kazakhstan started with a completely clean slate.

The country had to go through three principal changes: from a planned economy to a market-based one; from a one-party administrative system to a democratic one; and from traditional values to liberal ones. This demanded not just a radical dissolution of the entire

political and economic system, but also a swift abandonment of Soviet philosophies in general. Old habits die hard, and the new principles had to be almost forced through. This would prevent stagnation in the minds of a population apprehensive about change, overcome resistance from the old conservative order, and provide the reformers with the requisite knowledge and skills to sustain progress. Most difficult of all was instilling confidence in the voice of the people. They were still in shock from the breakdown of their once unshakeable system of values and confused by the need to make their own choices. People were reluctant to leave behind the illusory utopian ideals they held for the last seventy years. However, bringing them round to this radical yet exciting new reality was essential for Kazakhstan's development.

'How can you motivate a nation with no desire to motivate itself?' Nazarbayev would later write. 'How can you revitalize people whose brains have been filled for decades with an endless string of Marxist and Leninist maxims?' He too had once been a Soviet and understood how hard it was to rid oneself of established viewpoints, stereotypes and ways of life. But he also knew that without fundamental changes in the conscience of the people, there could be no future.

He repeated, like a personal mantra, one simple truth: only by trusting in one's own strength can an individual flourish, and no one – not the state, not society, not even one's peers – can help a person if he or she does nothing but prey on the mercy of others. Paternalism corrupts. Forcing people to seek out help robs them of their independence and their responsibility towards themselves and those around them. A powerful and prosperous state and a democratic society can be built only by a self-sufficient and self-reliant people.

Therefore he persistently tried to instill thoughts of personal success and responsibility into the people. If Soviet politics preached total ideological domination of the individual by the state, then Nazarbayev offered the opposite: a politics based on forming an independent personality, taking everything into one's own hands. Nazarbayev faced a dilemma: act gently and lose the momentum of change, or be decisive and tough, and risk social unrest.

He chose the second, less popular route, as in the chaotic conditions caused by the first years of independence, each delay could lead to collapse, and to the loss of sovereignty. One must not forget that there was a third, more traditional option available to Nazarbayev: to strengthen his own power and leave the country in its current state. But choosing this route would have contradicted his key aim: the construction of a modern state that was competitive in the globalizing world. He once said of Mikhail Gorbachev that though he had great power, he still strove for change – nothing better defines the credo of Nazarbayev.

Aiming to define the key pillars of development and the means to achieve them, Nazarbayev penned two theses – *Strategy for the Formation and Development of Kazakhstan as a Sovereign State* (1992), and *The Ideological Consolidation of Society as a Condition of Kazakhstan's Progress* (1993) – which would become the first works on the theory of state-building in Kazakhstan and were precursors to the Kazakhstan-2030 Strategy. It is no coincidence that Nazarbayev was the author of these works. He had been developing a serious interest in theoretical understanding and scientific analysis even in his years of studying at the Karaganda Polytechnic Institute. Building on his experience of working in the Karaganda Metallurgical Plant, he raised the question of how to recycle materials formed during ore processing. 'Kazakhstan is a rich and productive country,' he would go on to write in his book *Without Right and Left*, explaining his interest in this issue. 'But as the country has developed we have allowed it continue to be the norm that billions of tonnes of various mineral resources are left just lying around. This includes iron, cobalt, vanadium and nickel. Nowhere else in the world would allow such a careless and wasteful attitude to invaluable raw minerals. We make no use of these readily available recyclable resources, this treasure under our noses, even though extracting their valuable components would be considerably easier and a great deal cheaper than obtaining those same materials from the earth.

'This issue of recycling raw materials does not only concern mineral resources. For example, the oil fields of East Kazakhstan contain sulphur, as well as a huge number of gas condensates. From them one could produce polymers that would bring great profit to the country. And because we have not developed a complex agricultural production system, we not only lose what we grow but fail to make use of the other resources that could increase food production. For example, the use of the waste from the flour milling industry could be used in meat production.'

Nazarbayev had published numerous articles on these subjects over the years, such as 'Stages of Growth' in the *Economic Newspaper*, (18 August 1980), 'Wealth From Waste' in *Pravda* (10 September 1982), 'Necessities For Intensification' in *Pravda* (22 May 1983), 'Making Use Of One's Resources' in *Socialist Industry* (10 September 1983), amongst others. One can trace Nazarbayev's interest in recyclable materials back to his doctoral thesis *The Economic Potential of Natural Resources (in Kazakh Materials)*, completed in July 1990, and then to his postdoctoral thesis *Conservation Strategies in the Formation and Development of Market Relations*, which he successfully defended at the Russian Academy of Management in December 1992.

Meanwhile in the 'Strategy for the Formation and Development of Kazakhstan as a Sovereign State' and 'The Ideological Consolidation of Society as a Condition of Kazakhstan's Progress', Nazarbayev created a blueprint for the country's future – a continental model to develop Kazakhstan as an open society, and a democratic, peaceable state, which, as indicated in the Formation Strategy, ought to be:

(a) A strong presidential republic, which guarantees the rights and freedoms of its people, with political and ideological pluralism, ensuring internal and international harmony, stable defence and security, and an equal standing in the international community.

(b) Based upon a developed market economy with diverse forms of property and socially responsible entrepreneurship, healthy competition, and prudent contribution from foreign investors.

(c) With a clear social orientation, creating for every man without exception equal conditions and opportunities to apply his abilities for a materially prosperous existence, maintaining national consensus as a basis for stable development.

The need to offer solutions to challenges of this scale demanded an effectively structured government which could bring together and mobilize society. An attempt was made to fill the power vacuum left by the departed Communist Party with a Council of Deputies, headed by a Supreme Council. The Supreme Council was a Western-style Parliament, but in fact, having been the political foundation of the Soviet system, it became the core of the anti-reformist front. Deputies blocked any reforms proposed by the President and his government. The deputies continually made populist decisions to raise salaries and create unfunded social programmes, while the executive power bore responsibility for them despite the harsh budget deficit. Such measures, adopted at a time when the economy was failing and the treasury was empty, would come to be the cause of long-term debt with regard to social benefits. In addition, they failed to create a mechanism to regulate legal policy during the development of a market economy and democratic society, further hindering Kazakhstan's development.

Knowing this, Nazarbayev was personally involved in all sessions of the Supreme Council concerning key state issues; thus, the more significant the reform, the more violent the battles were, with reformists rallying around the President, and against the anti-reformists. The existing system of councils, with the Supreme Council at its head, ran contrary to the fundamentals of democratic society – the principle of division of power. The stand-off between the Supreme Council and the President was the consequence of two irreconcilable ideologies: state control and leveling on the one hand, and free-market forces on the other. It was in this enfeebled government, frustrated by internal division and a weakened economy, that a state of dual authority came about. This divide left the whole state at hazard, and Nazarbayev knew that surrender to retrogressive forces would mean missing an historic opportunity for progress. The victory of the Supreme Council would lead to the loss of a unified strategic direction and a reversal of reforms and, as a consequence, to economic collapse and the loss of sovereignty.

Kofi Annan, the Secretary General of the UN, on a visit to Kazakhstan early in the new millennium.

Opposing the reforms only exacerbated the situation and exposed the councils' failure to meet the challenges of the growing socio-economic crisis and ensure the country's transition to a market economy. Despite having total power in their hands, the system of councils had actually done nothing but slow down Kazakhstan's development. The unavoidable need for reform manifested itself in the first Constitution of the Republic of Kazakhstan on 23 January 1993.

Discussion descended quickly into disputes relating to the fundamental principles of the country's political system. There was real danger of public debate escalating into open political conflict, with much of the population still unready for change. It was therefore inevitable that the development of the 1993 Constitution turned into an endless search for linguistic compromise, resulting in multiple opposing positions. Thus, the final text of the Constitution ended up overly broad, trying to include all of these positions. The new Constitution was meant to confirm Kazakhstan's sovereignty by law. But the Fundamental Law was tinged with compromise, largely reproducing the 1978 Constitution of Soviet Kazakhstan. A dual

119

power system had formed in the country that had virtually paralyzed its development and required speedy resolution.

Three years later Nazarbayev would say: 'This was a compromise which we were forced to make for the sake of social harmony. The Fundamental Law did not do everything society had expected of it. It was a compromise between a market economy and the remnants of a command economy, a compromise between the past and the future.'

As the socio-economic situation in the country continued to deteriorate, the existing system of dual power resulted in a parliamentary crisis, ending in the collapse of the system of councils and the self-dissolution of the Supreme Council's Twelfth Convocation. The collapse began with the destruction of the grassroots structures of government. One after another, district councils, and then regional councils, took the decision to relinquish power. Mandates were being assigned by most of the deputies in the Supreme Council, who understood the need to reform representative government through separating the divisions of state power, and improving parliamentary legislation with regards to its professionalism and efficiency. On 13 December 1993, the Supreme Council's Twelfth Convocation announced its own dissolution.

The fate of the Supreme Council's Thirteenth Convocation, elected on 7 March 1994 – the first professional Kazakh Parliament – also proved to be plagued by contradiction. It came into power in the most difficult period of state-building, when the separation of powers had not been completed, when the market economy was still fledgling, and when the status of President, Parliament and government were not fully defined. Having been in power for a little less than a year, on the 6 March 1995, it was recognized by the Constitutional Court as illegitimate because of serious violations of the law committed during the elections.

The Supreme Council, not ready to disband after operating for just a year, was readying itself to begin a war of laws with the Constitutional Court, and to introduce changes to the Constitution which could significantly limit the power of judges in favour of legislators. In this difficult time, in order to avoid clashes between the divisions of power, the President acted as guarantor of the rights and freedoms of his citizens, of the Constitution and of the laws of the Republic, and took the decision to dissolve Parliament, having signed the decree on 11 March 1995 'On Measures Arising From the Resolution of the Constitutional Court', which supported the court's decision and confirmed his commitment to democracy. In order to prevent further damage to the country, and save the government from total paralysis while finding a way out of the constitutional crisis, the President resorted to a referendum, publishing the corresponding decree on 25 March 1995: 'On the Holding of a National Referendum on 29 April 1995'. Following the decree, the question emerged of extending the President's power until the 1 of December 2000, giving Nazarbayev special authority over the reformation of Kazakhstan. The results of the referendum were a convincing proof that the Kazakh people supported the plan for further change: 7,982,834 citizens were in favour of the extension of his power, 95.46 per cent of voters.

With national support obtained, the Head of State, in the absence of the supreme legislative body, was himself responsible for making legislation. Using the authority previously granted to him by the Supreme Council in a short time he managed to create an impressive legal framework. All in all about 140 presidential decrees were published using the force of the law, with more than sixty decrees on the ratification of international treaties.

At the same time the President had to draw up a new Constitution, the need for which had already been a top priority in Kazakhstan for quite some time. The 1995 Constitution was Nazarbayev's brainchild, and he was actively involved from its conception to the adoption of the Fundamental Law.

In Spring 1995 a working group was formed on his behalf, consisting of Kazakhstan's leading jurisprudents and a number of foreign experts, with N.A. Shaikenov as the group's head. Others included Y.G. Basin, V.A. Kim, K.A. Kolpakov, A.K. Kotov, B.A. Mukhamedzhanov, E.K. Nurpeisov, G.S. Sapargaliev, M.K. Suleimenov, and, of the foreign experts, S.S. Alekseev, J. Attali, and R. Dyuma. Nazarbayev assembled these names himself and, as the project neared its end, also invited various other specialists: historians, political scientists, ethnologists, linguists, journalists and so on.

As Nazarbayev saw it, Kazakhstan's new Constitution needed to incorporate everything advanced, effective and promising about constitutional law in other countries, but at the same time have its own style. And so it was up to the working group to locate this golden mean, a text for the future that must not be a rushed plagiarism of its foreign counterparts, or an antiquated hotchpotch of historical and ethnographic relics.

The President was keen to be at the very heart of brainstorming. He played a key role in comparing and contrasting the constitutions of dozens of countries in the development of a Fundamental Law, which also had to avoid ambiguities and legal disputes and lay down firm, long-term bases for a governing body. He ensured no stone was left unturned: every article, suggestion or even choice of wording was subject to scrutiny. So it was that they came to have a document which had passed through the hands of an army of specialists and been validated by all of them. Nazarbayev was also adamant that the Kazakh and Russian versions of the text were exactly identical, and so close attention was paid not only to the formal legal aspects of the text, but also to its lexis and grammar.

During the discussions Nazarbayev practically adopted the Stanislavski system, waiting till dispute was in full flow before interjecting forcefully: 'I don't believe you! Prove to me that it is so!' Following that, he would tend to record his opponents' arguments in a notebook, scribbling them away as if they were a thesis. Sometimes, late into to the night, when a debate seemed to have come to nothing, the President would bring the discussion to a close, bid everyone goodnight, and go home with the transcript of the debate, returning in the morning with a completed edition of the article they had been disputing.

In the Museum Of The First President you can find more than a dozen of these notebooks as well as various other heavily annotated papers of Nazarbayev's, which serve as a unique testimony to the work he put in to the creation of the Constitution.

Finally, on 4 June 1995, the project was published in the mass media for national discussion, which continued until the end of the month. Amendments were made in fifty-five of its ninety-eight articles, after which the Constitution draft was put to a referendum.

The referendum took place on 30 August 1995: 8,091,715 citizens took part, or 90.58 per cent of the population. Out of them, 7,212,773 citizens, or 89.14 per cent, voted for the new Constitution of the Republic of Kazakhstan, which would come to resolve many issues of organization of government, ownership, rights, civic freedoms and so forth.

The new Constitution legislated a presidential form of government, necessary for maintaining the integrity and stability of Kazakhstan. At the same time, prescribed within the Fundamental Law was the key democratic principle of the division of power between the legislative, executive and judicial bodies. The Constitution clearly defined each of their spheres of activity, without any overlaps where one might attempt to usurp another's authority.

But most important of all was that the new Constitution laid the groundwork for reform. In this sense it became a turning point in the history of Kazakhstan, occupying a role as important as the obtaining of independence. A period of total modernization in the country began.

Meanwhile, equally important things were happening in the economic sphere. Kazakhstan had inherited an unbalanced economy from the Soviet Union, based purely on raw materials. The collapse of the Soviet Union brought with it terrible levels of unemployment, a deficit and hyperinflation. Industrial output halved, there was a drop of almost a third in agricultural production, and two-thirds in transportation. A flawed banking system paralyzed trade, with financial targets not being met for months. Debt equaled the Republic's GDP, interest rates on loans exceeded 400 per cent, and annual inflation disappeared off the scale (as far as 2500 per cent). And as industrial giants ground to a halt, more than half the country's businesses went bankrupt or ceased to make any financial gain.

The decline in production and the disappearance of the former channels of financial support drastically reduced incoming revenue. As a result, the average monthly wage more than halved, and the minimum wage dropped by nearly 90 per cent. Pensions, benefits and wages went unpaid: payments in kind and bartering became the norm. As if during the war, it was hunger and cold that were now the real dangers.

Ten years later, Nazarbayev painted Kazakhstan's position in these first years of independence thus: 'There can be no disguising the situation: I can tell you right now that at the start of the 1990s, we were standing at the edge of the abyss.'

The situation demanded immediate and decisive action for macroeconomic stabilization and a rapid transition to a market economy. The first step in this direction was the liberalization of prices, implemented in January 1992 with the aim of overcoming the acute shortage of commodities and rampant hyperinflation. Another of the priorities was to bring in measures to create an independent budget, tax and customs system.

However, the main condition for the transition to a market economy was the expansion of the private sector through the privatization of state property, the development of market infrastructure and the creation of a competitive market environment. This step was important both in involving the general populace more, and in instilling in them the concept of ownership.

There were several stages in this process: the programme of privatizing state property in the Kazakh Soviet Socialist Republic in 1991 and 1992, the programme privatizing state property in 1993 and 1994, and the programme of privatizing and restructuring state property in the Republic of Kazakhstan in 1996 and 1998. During the first phase of 1991 and 1992, state property was transferred to collective ownership based on how it could best be used. In total, about 4500 items were privatized, including 472 state farms.

In the second phase of 1993–95, the main emphasis was placed on the privatization of housing, service companies, trade, consumer services, utilities, and transport, as well as the privatization of the major industries and agro-industrial enterprises. In addition, this period saw the widespread application of coupon privatization, where all citizens were given free coupons to enable their participation in the privatization of the various items of state property.

Of course, on this basis the privatization was directed towards property that would produce income. But for former Soviet citizens, having one's own home was the most important thing of all – and so privatization functioned in the lives of ordinary Kazakhs primarily as a means to acquire private property from the public fund. This brought many people the security that was so crucial to surviving those difficult first years of independence.

In the third and final stage of 1996–98, large industrial enterprises became subject to privatization, most of all those in electricity, metallurgy, oil and gas.

Already, by the mid 1990s, these measures had started to bear fruit. The share of the private sector in the economy had reached 80 per cent, including 95 per cent in agriculture, 86 per cent in industry, 84 per cent in construction, and 56 per cent in transport. In total the amount of gross national product from the private sector increased to 50 per cent, including around 45 per cent in industry, 90 per cent in agriculture, 85 per cent in trade, and 60 per cent in construction. As a result, consumer goods saturated the market, and the queues disappeared.

The redirection of the country from socialism to capitalism required practical knowledge and Nazarbayev had to learn as he went along: 'In 1993 I invited Lee Kuan Yew to Kazakhstan, and spent a week by his side. Sometimes we would chat for five or six hours, and as I listened to him I would make notes. I had a few American advisers, and I paid close attention to everything they said. I had a representative of the International Monetary Fund working with me. It was like I was being

Above and right:
The joyless routine of daily life
in the early 1990s would become
a thing of the past.

reeducated, having to sit and read books on market economics and finance, like I was attending a whole new university course, where I studied the banking system, economics, politics, democracy, and freedom of speech, because I had received my education in an entirely different world.

'It was at this time, too, that he started to study spoken English. As German had been the foreign language of his school years, he had to learn English from scratch as if he was at primary school.

Up until the end of 1993, Kazakhstan, as it was in the common ruble zone, actually had no real opportunity to pursue an independent economic policy. However, given the close economic ties between the former Soviet republics, Nazarbayev supported a gradual, cautious concerted exit from the common ruble zone. In this regard, he initiated the signing of a large number of bilateral and multilateral Kazakh-Russian treaties with other CIS states, concerning mutual obligations

In a mood of spiritual revival, Nazarbayev and his First Lady greet the country's religious leaders – Muslim (left) and Christian (right).

to maintain the ruble zone until the member states introduced their own currencies. But the Russian government, convinced of the need to free itself as quickly as possible from ballast when it came to the Commonwealth states, tried to expel them from the ruble zone.

Realizing this, the President took proactive measures. To this end, in the spring of 1992, he secretly created a commission of seven people to plan and organize the introduction of a national currency. Non-disclosure agreements were made with every person involved. The design of the money was entrusted to a group of artists led by Timur Suleimenov, Nazarbayev would later recall in his book *At the Dawn Of the Twenty-first Century*. 'Work on introducing the national currency was not a solely stressful experience: there were plenty of cheerful moments. The first source of amusement was the proposal of a draft bill with my portrait on it: naturally, I rejected this option. We decided to put portraits of our great ancestors on the face-side of the draft bills, and, on the back, monuments of culture and nature: Western experts told us that these kind of images are difficult to forge. I approved the design for blueprints, which were then kept in a safe in England. The keys of this safe and the first samples of the money were brought to me. The business was complete; no one knew about it.

'In 1992, 20 per cent of the currency was printed just in case. No one found out about this. With the British we kept the whole operation secret. But to print even a little money, you need a complicated mathematic calculation – how many bills are needed, and

Nazarbayev greets the champion of economic freedom, Lee Kuan Yew of Singapore.

which ones? It fell to us to decide what exchange rate to set, and how to build relations with foreign partners. This was a very difficult economic and political question. A group of young economists were brought together to process all of these calculations, along with specialists from international financial bodies (the IMF, World Bank, the EBRD and so on).

'We also had a big argument over the naming of the currency. It was proposed that it be called "som", or "aksha". I preferred "altyn" or "tenge". These are terms understood by all peoples of the CIS, and

For the presidential image to appear on bank notes was a proposal rejected by the President himself.

which are also part of the Turkic and Slavic languages. We settled upon tenge.'

On 26 July 1993, despite official assurances to the contrary from its leaders, Russia took the unilateral decision to introduce its own currency, and began to replace the ruble banknotes issued between 1961 and 1992 with a new model of ruble. At the same time Kazakhstan found itself ejected from the ruble zone. In the Republic there was a massive discharge of old Soviet money, first from Kyrgyzstan, then from Russia.

In order to prevent financial collapse from threatening Kazakhstan, the President sped up the introduction of the national currency. 'We got and paid 7 million dollars the manufacturing costs for the remaining quantity of tenge,' Nazarbayev continues in the same book. 'We hired four IL-76 planes and brought in 60 per cent of the currency. It was a secret operation. The documents read: "Equipment for the Building of the Presidential Residence". By that point we had had underground warehouses built. Four planes made eighteen return flights in a week between London and Uralsk, and other regions of Kazakhstan. The hardest thing was getting the money delivered to each region and every bank. This was done in eight days. The world has probably never seen a new currency introduced so quickly and efficiently.

'I had made a prior warning about the introduction of the tenge to the leaders of our neighbour states, I.A. Karimov, A.A. Akayev, S.A. Niyazov. On the evening of 12 November, I appeared on national television and announced the transition to the new currency. As had been agreed beforehand, President Karimov announced the introduction of the som in Uzbekistan on the same day and at the same time.'

In accordance with the presidential decree 'On the Introduction of the National Currency of the Republic of Kazakhstan' on 15 November 1993, the tenge came into circulation at a rate of 1 tenge to 500 Soviet rubles. This day became the official Day of National Currency.

With the introduction of the tenge Kazakhstan gained economic independence, and finally secured its sovereignty, which had been proclaimed on 16 December 1991. The move to its own currency also allowed it to curb hyperinflation, which was halved to 1260 per cent in 1994 and by the end of 1995 had gone all the way down to 58 per cent.

Nazarbayev was only able to rally the Kazakh people around him through tolerance and genuine internationalism, fostered throughout

The true value of economic sovereignty is the country's wealth.

his life. These features showed themselves more than ever in those first, most difficult years of independence. At that time in Kazakhstan, just as in the other former Soviet republics, ethnic tensions were at breaking point. In the early 1990s this already delicate balance looked increasingly likely to be disrupted.

Calmly assessing the impending dangers and plotting some kind of resolution, the President assembled every state-governing resource at his disposal and sent trustworthy men into the problem areas. When necessary he himself went to conflict zones to hear his citizens' demands and speak directly with them. During these trips, Nazarbayev frequently found himself caught in the crossfire between nationalists and radical representatives of ethnic minorities.

As the draft of the Constitution was discussed by the people, the fiercest debates concerned the questions of State language and dual citizenship. As such, Nazarbayev settled the matter by supporting the use of Russian and Kazakh, presenting this in an address to the people. The President stressed that most crucial was the salvation of the Kazakh language, which was teetering on the brink of extinction. But, on the other hand, linguistic policy was to ensure respect for the Russian language, as well as other languages, as a means of international communication. The proposition he put forward calmed the storm and led to a breakthrough in this area.

Common sense also prevailed regarding the question of dual citizenship. As the Soviet Union disintegrated, multiple grudges had arisen between its former republics over territory and property, and both outside and inside Kazakhstan there were fervent political separatist groups calling for a redrawing of its boundaries. Nazarbayev therefore identified international harmony from the very beginning as a basic principle of state policy. He based this on the principle of 'unity in diversity', an attempt to consolidate the Kazakh people into an ethnic culture genetically linked to the Kazakh territory. Many countries and scientific doctrines might have considered such polyethnicity as an explosion waiting to happen, but Nazarbayev had been set on destroying this notion since the late 1980s, considering the ethnic and linguistic mosaic of the state to be invaluable social and humanitarian capital, and a key factor in Kazakhstan's progress.

The origins of the Kazakh leader's worldview are to be found in his childhood. The polyethnic environment of his native Chemolgan, his time studying in the Ukrainian city of Dneprodzerzhinsk, and his work in a multinational company at Karmetkombinat, all taught him to treat people primarily based on their actions and their character, not on their nationality. He writes about this in his book *Without Right and Left*: 'There were usually six to eight people on rotation in the blast furnace, and one rarely encountered more than two or three people of a single nationality in any one group. In our team, I was the only Kazakh, and besides me there was a Tatar, a Russian, a Ukrainian … A man's worth was defined not by his nationality, but by totally different qualities which were very quickly revealed by this kind of work.'

Encouraging a climate of tolerance and harmony, Nazarbayev never forgot that Kazakhstan was the historic land of the Kazakhs, who for many years were forced to be outcasts in their own land. And so from the very first years of independence the process of returning those repatriates who had once been forced to leave their home to Kazakhstan began. The reunification of this ethnic diaspora started decisively at the first World Congress of Kazakhs in 1992, attended by over 700 delegates from more than thirty countries. Today Kazakhstan is one of only three countries in the world with a policy of bringing its compatriots back from abroad, and during the years of independence around a million people have returned.

So it was that independence brought unprecedented opportunities for a real national rebirth for Kazakhstan.

On 4 June 1992, Kazakhstan gained its own state symbols – a state flag, a state coat of arms and a state anthem. After centuries and decades of neglect, the people had the names and relics they held dear returned to them: their dignity and their pride in their history, and their ancestors, was restored.

In May 1993, on the initiative of the President, grand celebrations were held at the foot of a mountain in Ordabasy in South Kazakhstan

A fresh design for the national flag of Kazakhstan is displayed for evaluation.

At the 150th anniversary of the birth of Abay Kunanbayev the President is visited by UNESCO General Director, Federico Mayor Zaragoza.

– a historic place for the Kazakh people. It was here that, in one of the country's darkest hours, Aktaban Shubyryndy, the Kazakh hordes, inspired by their famous sons – the sages *biys* Tole Bi, Kazybek Bi and Aiteke Bi – first united to fight the Jungar invaders for the independence and territorial integrity of the motherland.

Participating in the celebrations were about 100,000 residents of Southern Kazakhstan, delegations from all regions of the country, the cities of Almaty and Leninsk, and also from Kyrgyzstan, Tajikistan, Turkmenistan, Uzbekistan and other CIS countries. The guests of honour at the celebration were the presidents of Uzbekistan, I.A. Karimov, and Kyrgyzstan, A.A. Akayev.

Addressing the gathering, Nazarbayev stressed that the heroic life and deeds of the three great *biys* taught a lesson worth following. 'The wise *biys* managed to bring a simple and yet a great truth into our consciousness,' he said, 'a powerful motivating force for growth is the desire of the public, the common goal against which every practical step must be measured. If at the time of the glorious Tole Bi, Kazybek Bi and Aiteke Bi, the greatest concern was the unity of all Kazakhs, so today must the the Kazakh people, united by our holy ancestors, work towards the unification of everyone who inhabits this country. To achieve this end we must unite all the people of our republic into one single family, and ensure all our efforts in achieving this are united too. This simple formula must take deep root in the minds of today's citizens, who represent many nationalities, and many generations to come.'

Other major events in public life were those organized in memory of prominent historical figures who had died under Stalinist repression – T. Ryskulov, S. Khodzhanov, S. Seyfullin, I. Dzhansugurov, and B. Mailin – and heroes of the events of December 1986, but the crowning glory of these events were the celebrations held in 1995 to mark the 150th anniversary of the great Kazakh poet, thinker and public figure Abay Kunanbayev.

In line with Nazarbayev's ethnic policy, the Assembly of the People of Kazakhstan was created on 1 March 1995, a structure with no international parallel, designed to bring the country's President and his people closer together.

The President revealed what would be the universal and enduring role of the Assembly in the early years of its existence: 'Mutual understanding is not restricted to the first and second five-year periods of independence, nor a matter of naked political pragmatism. We must learn and pass on to the next generation two simple truths: Kazakhstan will always be a multiethnic state, and one which will never bear witness to ethnic cleansing; our polyethnicity is a huge cultural, economic and political resource. Our task is a simple one – we all need to feel a sense of civic community. But there are great difficulties behind this too: nostalgia for the past, and the many prejudices of the old and young brother. The sooner we recognize the new political reality of independent Kazakhstan, the sooner every man will sense his role in shaping his own destiny, and the longer our national harmony will last.'

The balanced approach of the President became one of the major factors enabling Kazakhstan to remain stable, even against a global backdrop of multiple ethnic and religious wars. Indeed Nazarbayev considers this one of his greatest achievements.

Another national project of great strategic importance to be achieved in the first years of independence was initiated by Nazarbayev in 1993: the Bolashak Programme, the state-funded system of higher education for the young and talented of Kazakhstan in the very best foreign universities. Unique in its design, and the first training programme of its kind in the CIS, it has proved extremely successful, granting students great social prestige and guaranteeing professional fulfilment and career success for its graduates. Many Bolashakers are now successfully employed in various government posts. Later, at the very end of the 2000s, Nazarbayev University was opened, designed to become a leading scientific, educational and research centre of international repute, as well as a centre for various schools of thought. With regard to this, the

President has repeatedly emphasized that educational policy is one of the most important of the state's breakthrough projects, aimed at creating a modern and competitive nation.

From the very first days of independence, Nazarbayev led an active multifaceted policy to see Kazakhstan recognized by the international community, in order to ensure its stability and to establish beneficial economic relations. Kazakhstan's independence was recognized first by Turkey, and then by the vast majority of the worlds countries. Over time, it would complete the process of establishing diplomatic relations with foreign countries. At the same time, Kazakhstan began cooperating with powerful international organizations, including the UN, the OSCE, the EU, the IMF, the World Bank, the EBRD (European Bank for Reconstruction and Development), UNESCO, UNICEF, UNEP, ESCAP (the Economic and Social Commission for Asia and the Pacific), the UNDP (United Nations Development Programme), the World Health Organization, the IAEA (International Atomic Energy Agency), the OIC (Organization of the Islamic Conference), and others. On 2 January 1992, Kazakhstan became a member of the Organization for Security and Cooperation in Europe, and on 3 March 1992 was admitted to the United Nations.

Nazarbayev made use of every opportunity to achieve these goals, including making appearances at international events. From the very beginning the Kazakh leader shied away from the small-town mindset characteristic of most developing countries, and positioned Kazakhstan strongly within the global picture. With this frame of mind he proposed a number of major international initiatives to the global community. For example, at the fourth-seventh session of the UN General Assembly in October 1992, Nazarbayev came out with an initiative to call for a Conference on Interaction and Confidence Building Measures in Asia (CICA): 'The idea of creating a structure for security and cooperation in Asia along the lines of the CSCE in Europe has been talked about for a long time … The transition to this kind of continental structure can be achieved through a gradual, step-by-step process: starting with bilateral relations between regional coalitions (in pursuit of trust and collective security, based on humanitarian, economic and cultural interaction) all the way up to continental bodies for cooperation on a wider range of problems.'

Nazarbayev announced another initiative on 29 March 1994, at Lomonosov Moscow State University: the idea of a Eurasian Union. 'Unfortunately, today the CIS does not fully meet the objective

The Head of State with Kazakhstan's First Minister of Defence, Hero of the Soviet Union Sagadat Nurmagambetov.

requirements of the age and does not enable the integration of its member countries, which is so desperately needed by our people. There is now an urgent need for a transition to an essentially new kind of relationship between our countries on the basis of a new interstate unit, formed on the principles of free will and equal rights. This association could become a Eurasian Union (EAU). It should be based on different principles to the CIS, for the basis of this organization should be to create supranational bodies to then resolve two key problems: the formation of a single economic space and the ensuring of a common defence policy. It is important to stress that all other matters concerning the interests of sovereignty, the domestic state-political body, and the foreign policy of each party, should remain unaffected, and interference in one anothers internal affairs ought to be avoided.'

Both of these initiatives went on to be developed and implemented. And, indeed, the idea of a Eurasian Union was the basis for future international bodies in the post-Soviet area, such as the Common Economic Space (CES), the Eurasian Economic Community (EurAsEC), the Customs Union of Belarus, Kazakhstan and Russia, and finally the Eurasian Economic Union, whose establishment agreement was signed by the leaders of the three countries, D.A. Medvedev, Nazarbayev, and A.G. Lukashenko, on 18 November 2011.

Always careful to uphold regional security and cooperation, the President simultaneously paid great attention to the creation of Kazakhstan's armed forces. After the collapse of the USSR, many officers and soldiers of the Soviet Army, divided by the new state boundaries, were

The Supreme Commander of the 149th regiment of Kazakhstan's Air Force, September 1995.

disorientated and demoralized. Because of this, and moreover due to the complications caused by the economic crisis, discipline amongst the troops dropped disastrously. Therefore, from the first days of independence, these questions surrounding the armed forces became one of Nazarbayev's central concerns.

On 10 January 1992, at the Security Council, the President begun to develop the country's military, commissioning an inventory of technology, weapons, ammunition and other general military equipment, and proposing the creation of multidisciplinary military schools. On the same day he met with commanding officers and assured them: 'The army will not be left to deal with its problems alone. On my instructions, a decree is being prepared on the social protection of servicemen.

'We cannot allow a collapse in the management of military bodies, nor confusion in the process of transforming the armed forces,' Nazarbayev elaborated at a meeting on 12 January with the Commander of the Joint Armed Forces of the CIS, Marshal E.I. Shaposhnikov and the Commander of the Turkestan Military District. And on 13 January he met with the heads of the country's defence organizations, to discuss the

support and development of the defence industry. The President highlighted the issue again on 16 January in Moscow, where he had come to take part in an army officers' conference.

The effort put in by the Head of State during the winter and spring of 1992 brought clarity to the question of army's fate, and most importantly prevented military equipment, including nuclear, chemical and biological weapons, from falling into criminal hands.

On 7 May 1992, Nazarbayev signed the decree 'On the Creation of the Armed Forces of the Republic of Kazakhstan'. During the course of 1992 and 1993 the Republican Guard, the Ground Forces (internal and border troops), and the Naval Forces were formed. During this unpredictable and dangerous period the President directly oversaw the establishment of the armed forces of independent Kazakhstan, another step towards sovereignty, strengthening Kazakhstan's defences and enhancing its international authority.

Making a speech on the fifth anniversary of Kazakhstan's independence, Nazarbayev summed up the nation's achievements over the period thus: 'Few nations have had to overcome such complex problems in such a short period of time. Building a strong state and an effective economy whilst also maintaining ethnic harmony and political stability is the challenge that we have been set, right at the very turn of the century: never before in this country's history has there been this chance to create a state that could last for centuries. It is up to our generation to capitalize on this precious opportunity.'

As a result of this anniversary Nazarbayev achieved a key political victory: the adoption of the Fundamental Law. At the ceremony officially presenting the new Constitution of Kazakhstan, the result of the republican referendum of 30 August 1995, he announced: 'Following the example of the constitutions of many democratic countries, this Constitution shall serve as a solid legal structure on which we can build and develop a modern state and a market economy.'

Opposite:
In the creation of the independent Republic of Kazakhstan, the formalities of state and constitutional vows have been honoured with unfailing solemnity.

8

Strategy for Growth

The 1995 Constitution was the start of a new chapter in the country's development. It marked the end of the initial stage of Kazakh independence, and set in motion systemic reforms in all spheres of society.

There had been dramatic changes to the configuration of the organs of state power. Under the Constitution state power is unified, conforming to the principle of separating the legislative, executive and judicial branches which cooperate by a system of checks and balances. The Constitution clearly outlined the sphere of influence of each branch of power. In principle, the presidential institution gained a new status, functioning as a kind of a referee between them.

Among Kazakhstan's multiple mineral endowments, its oil and gas was to prove most valuable as the economy was opened up to the vigour and competitive disciplines of the free market.

This position was effected by leverage upon all three branches; most importantly the President had the right to dissolve Parliament and the government was answerable to him. The judicial system was reformed, and a Constitutional Council created. The former Soviet system of representative bodies was replaced by the newly operating bicameral Parliament.

At the opening of the first session of his first Parliament, the country's President, before a joint meeting of Senate and Majilis [lower house of Parliament] deputies, made note of the fact that there were modern Kazakhs present for this moment, which he intended to be a significant chapter in both the country's annals and in the history of the development of the state. They were witnessing the birth of a Kazakh parliamentary system which he believed to be civilized and proper. It was

Above:
The youthful President lays out the policies of the new Kazakhstan.

Left:
Attracting investors –
the key strategic priority.

the first time in the operations of the State Parliament that it was divided into upper and lower chambers. In that same Parliament there now exists a system of counterweights that supposedly increase the degree to which MPs are able to interact and make demands of one another, and thus reduce the chances of making 'raw' laws. Parliament's main political task, which had to be a constant no matter what area of legislation, was to consolidate positive legislation to date, and conclusively stabilize the political, economic and social climate for the country to move forward. Thus it was that the Basic Law of 1995 and the power structure implemented alongside it restored stability to the state.

Economic reforms meanwhile continued. The second half of the 1990s was marked by the stabilization of the main macroeconomic indicators and the creation of dynamic conditions in which progressive structural changes, national economic growth, and the integration of Kazakhstan into the global economy could occur. The declining production ceased, the country significantly reduced its rate of inflation, and for the first time in many years ensured a growth in GDP, which in 1997 reached 2 per cent. Industrial production rose to 4 per cent. The national monetary system, based on the Kazakh tenge, was regaining its strength.

And so began the transition to specific programmes for strategic economic sectors, including oil and gas, metal and electrical power. Given the lack of funds to kick-start the process of turning these resources' economic potential into profit, foreign investment needed to be attracted, investment which could not only solve the problem of financing the operation but would provide the experience and technology so sorely lacking. Were this not to be achieved, the country would stay trapped in its vicious circle of problems: the steep decline in

Right:
Kazakhstan's launching site for the exploration of space in Baikonur.

Exemplifying the confidence and promise of the newly independent Kazakhstan, the President pays allegiance to Kazakhs of the past.

production, the paralysis of its industrial giants, credit shortages and lack of capital for investment, inflation, low levels of revenue and rising unemployment.

With this in mind, great effort was made to create a favourable climate for investment. As the business world of the West had no idea of whether Kazakhstan would make a viable and reliable economic partner, Nazarbayev personally visited each of the world's most important countries to represent his country and discuss its investment potential. The Presidential Council was created for foreign investors, which included the leaders of all the world's largest multinational corporations. These investors were offered special privileges which exempted them from payment of income tax, land tax, property tax and customs duties, and provided with guarantees to cover their political and regulatory risks. Among the many other attractions of the investment climate was its assurance against expropriation, convertibility of currency, consent to international mediation, guarantee of legal stability, transparency of governmental dealings, and continued development of priority sectors.

The oil and gas sector was the pioneer in attracting foreign investment. There had already been some positive progress in this area. In the late 1980s, in the twilight of the Soviet Union, Nazarbayev had

143

Out on the steppe with children.

taken part in some preliminary talks with America, which led to the creation, with Chevron, of a joint Kazakh-American company Tengizchevroil (TCO) in 1993. Chevron became the first foreign oil company to come to work in Kazakhstan, and the contract that was drawn up over this was the largest in the entire post-Soviet area.

Nazarbayev once said: 'Oil usually offers us either wealth, or blood. For this oil giant to function, we need not only pipelines but political solutions.' He was now expected to provide these solutions. To attract investors, he had to take the responsibility for making concessions concerning property rights and allowing the purchase of major shareholdings in the oil companies. In these difficult socio-political conditions it was difficult to determine whether privatization would bring potentially huge profit, or be extremely costly to a key constituent

Connecting with China – the birth of the Shanghai Cooperation Organization is marked with a collective handshake.

Right:
Former President of the US,
George Bush Sr., played host
to Nazarbayev.

of the economy. There was a great risk that control over one of the country's key strategic resources would be surrendered, which would pose a direct threat to national autonomy. However, the country found itself with no other option: Nazarbayev made the decision to turn the country's oil and gas reserves into a resource of the free-market.

As a result, the industry sprang to life, and production began to increase, reaching 30.6 million tonnes of oil and 4.7 million tonnes of condensate (693,000 barrels per day) by 2000. In general, at the turn of the century, oil production in the country was increasing at an average rate of 16 per cent per year, leading Nazarbayev to set the ambitious target of becoming one of the world's top ten oil exporters in the not too distant future. The boom in oil production largely ensured that Kazakhstan's economy would continue to grow at a rapid rate.

However, further expansion of oil and gas production was seriously hindered by the unsettled question of the legal status of the Caspian Sea, which was believed to be have the second biggest potential energy reserves in the world. At the time of the collapse of the Soviet Union, the legal status of the Caspian Sea was defined by the Soviet-Iranian agreements of 1921 and 1940. According to these, Iran and Russia, as the legal successors of the USSR, were recognized as the Caspian Sea's only coastal states, and as such formed a condominium with exclusive dominion over its waters, seabed and resources. However, after the collapse of the Soviet Union and the emergence in the Caspian region of new states in the form of Azerbaijan, Kazakhstan and Turkmenistan, the established order was in need of complete revision.

The negotiations were tense from the beginning. While Russia and Iran maintained that a change to the established regulation would be inappropriate, the new claimants invoked their rights, and appealed to international maritime law, on the basis of which they demanded that the Caspian sectors should be divided along a median line, giving each country a share proportional to the length of its coastline. In turn, Russia and Iran insisted that the Caspian Sea was not a sea, but rather an inland lake, and therefore that it was not subject to international maritime law. Iran later proposed an alternative of dividing the area equally between the five littoral states. However, this was contradictory to the interests of the other countries, including Russia, and so the negotiations came to nothing for a long time.

In this situation, Kazakhstan, taking into account that the main oil reserves were concentrated in the northern part of the sea, focused on negotiating with Russia. However, the Russians refused to budge from their earlier position and only after the intervention of Nazarbayev, who conducted a one-on-one negotiation with President Boris Yeltsin in July 1998, that breakthrough was finally made. During this meeting, which went on for many tense hours, Nazarbayev was able to convince his Russian counterpart to divide the sea bed between the two countries along the median line, and offered mutually beneficial resolutions to the numerous issues this threw up. In particular, the parties agreed on the correction of the path of the median line in one area to benefit Russia, and on the joint exploitation of the deposits at Khvalynskoe and Tsentralnoe. All this was outlined in the 'Agreement on the Delimitation of the Caspian Seabed' on 6 July 1998.

Following the example of this contract, in September 2002 Kazakhstan and Azerbaijan approved a bilateral agreement on the delimitation of their adjacent sections of the northern part of the Caspian Sea, and in May 2003 the two countries signed a tripartite agreement with Russia, which established geographic coordinates to clearly define the dividing lines, and the limited parts of the sea bed within which the parties could exercise their sovereign rights for exploring and mining mineral resources. These agreements ended decades of political and legal disputes over the northern part of the Caspian Sea and opened up whole new areas of opportunity for the intensive development of Caspian energy resources.

Another problem which had long been a headache for the Kazakh authorities until the resolution of the Caspian Sea issue was Baikonur. The collapse of the Soviet Union and the subsequent economic crisis

The hydrocarbon industry is centred upon the Caspian region.

had left the fate of Baikonur, the cosmodrome that had come into Kazakh ownership on 31 August 1991, as an ongoing problem. In these crisis conditions the upkeep of Baikonur, which required huge investment, remained an enormous burden on the shoulders of the new state. In turn, Russia, forced by its own economic situation to make cuts in its space programme, seriously considered relinquishing the cosmodrome. In those difficult years, due to poor living conditions and lack of confidence in its future, Baikonur had been abandoned by the thousands of highly qualified specialists who had created it. However, at the same time the President was acutely aware of the importance of preserving this unique space complex. Understanding that man cannot live on bread alone, and that one must look beyond the everyday and into the future, he understood the value of Baikonur and searched long and hard for a solution to the crisis. 'We ought to see Baikonur as the potential domestic centre for our space activity and even for the formation of a whole space industry.' It was Nazarbayev's vision that this industry might one day become one of the cornerstones of an innovative Kazakh economy. It was clear that Kazakhstan alone was not equipped to meet this challenge. Only a collaborative effort could save the cosmodrome, and the idea of building an international space consortium with Baikonur at its centre appeared a feasible solution.

Thus Kazakhstan began an active search for international partners. The President assigned this task to the Space Research Institute, formed in 1991, and then to the National Space Agency that replaced it. But much time passed without any real progress. In the end, it so happened that the solution came about incidentally. In 1994, two documents were signed by Kazakhstan and Russia that proved critical for Baikonur – the Agreement on the Basic Conditions for Use of the Baikonur Complex on 28 March, and the Agreement on the Lease of the Baikonur Complex on 10 December. According to these documents, the space complex was leased to Russia for twenty years. On 9 January 2004, the lease was extended until 2050.

And so Baikonur was reborn – but only after a difficult negotiation process. The Baikonur problem, just like the Caspian problem, was an extremely sensitive one, since Russia, as the legal successor of the USSR, considered the spaceport its baby.

Again, only through becoming personally involved could Nazarbayev save the situation. As the negotiations neared completion, and the question of annual rent arose, he made the following suggestion to Yeltsin: 'How about a symbolic rent of 100 million dollars a year?' He then jokingly added 'And another 15 million as a sign of our friendship.' 'That seems fair to me,' Yeltsin replied, appreciating the humour but considering the price fair. Thus did Kazakhstan and Russia's mutually respectful approach to solving the problem of the Baikonur complex allow the spaceport to regain its global status.

Today the cosmodrome is one of the leading international spaceports, third in the world in terms of the number of space launches, and accounting for more than a quarter of global launches. More than 70 per cent of Russian space programmes, and many more international ones, are connected to the spaceport.

Another issue inherited from the former Soviet Union in the 1990s was the urgent need for Kazakhstan to define its borders with its neighbouring states, of which one of the most serious was China. The border stretched for 1740 kilometers and Kazakhstan was the first Central Asian state to settle its territorial issues with them. The treaty 'On the Kazakh-Chinese Border', agreed in April 1994, defined the course of the boundary in its entirety, with the exception of two disputed areas – near the Sary-Cheldiev River (in the Almaty region) and the Chagan-Obo and Baymurza passes (in the former Semipalatinsk region). For these, additional agreements were signed on 24 September 1997 and 4 July 1998, under which 407 square kilometres of these disputed areas went to China, and 537 square miles remained with Kazakhstan. The success of the negotiation process was down largely to the tactics chosen by Nazarbayev, as he made the bilateral negotiations multilateral, involving all the stakeholders in the form of a joint delegation of former Soviet republics including Kazakhstan, Russia, China, Kyrgyzstan and Tajikistan.

A special relationship: Nazarbayev with Jiang Zemin of China and Vladimir Putin of Russia.

After lengthy negotiations, on 26 April 1996 in Shanghai, the five states celebrated the signing of an agreement of trust regarding a military region of the border area, an unparalleled event in international relations. From that moment a new phase of relations with China began, founded on the principles of mutual trust and cooperation. Later, on 24 April 1997, the presidents of the five countries signed a new mutual agreement to cut back their armies' presence in the border region.

Thus, until 2020, the two agreements provided a solid foundation for stability and for close cooperation through regional organizations such as the Shanghai Five and the Shanghai Cooperation Organization (SCO). Indeed, on a treaty basis, by the mid 2000s Kazakhstan would settle territorial disputes with its neighbours, above all with Russia and China, agreements that Kazakh historians call the 'contracts of the century'.

Throughout these various complex disputes, President Nazarbayev was careful to maintain warm and trusting relationships with the leaders of other major countries and international organizations. Of course, Kazakhstan's diplomatic success cannot be ascribed solely to amicable meetings between heads of state. But there is no doubt that international relations can be improved by friendship between politicians, as Nazarbayev illustrated.

The events of June 2002 are revealing in this respect, when the first summit of the Conference on Interaction and Confidence Building Measures in Asia (CICA) took place in Almaty. Immediately after the summit, Nazarbayev invited the heads of Kazakhstan's two most

Above:
On board the presidential airplane.

Left:
Cross-border companionship: Nazarbayev with the President of Tajikistan, Emomalii Rahmon (left) and of Uzbekistan, Islam Karimov (right).

formidable neighbours – the Chinese President Jiang Zemin and the Russian President Vladimir Putin – to his home. One rarely sees the heads of even the most amicable states welcoming one another to the table of their family home. From the beginning of his tenure as President, Nazarbayev had the strength of character and courage in his convictions to stay faithful to the hospitable traditions of the steppe.

In the early 1990s, US Vice President Al Gore made a visit to Kazakhstan. After official business was done, the President invited the Vice President to his home. To Gore's delight, Kazakh custom dictated that the host give his guest a sheep's head, and then play a few songs on the dombra. Politicians after all are still people, and nothing impresses others so much as the joy of shared experience.

Kazakh television showed a small but revealing report on the visit of Jiang Zemin and Vladimir Putin to the President's house. Nazarbayev presented his guests with a small hand-held dagger, joking: 'May this serve you as a weapon against terrorists.' There was sense behind this gift: the main topic of conversation at the CICA summit in Almaty, held eight months after the attacks of 11 September in the US, had been their shared opposition to international terrorism. Nazarbayev developed the warmest relationship with Chinese leader Jiang Zemin, which proved an important factor in the development of Kazakh-Chinese relations. Because they both spoke Russian they could communicate without interpreters. They also both loved to sing and play musical instruments. Their shared repertoire included the popular Soviet song 'Moscow Nights' and the famous Kazakh folk song 'Dudarai'.

Left:
A meeting of old friends:
Nursultan Nazarbayev with
Boris Yeltsin of Russia.

The personal friendship between Nazarbayev and the Russian President Boris Yeltsin also lasted for many years. Having made his acquaintance during the Soviet era, Nazarbayev had always had a close and trusting relationship with Yeltsin. They were regularly brought together by their official duties, and together resolved many disputes between the two countries. This relationship did not come to an end when Yeltsin left office. The Kazakh President, far from severing ties, would speak regularly to his friend on the phone and find time to see him whenever he made an official visit to Moscow. When Nazarbayev won a landslide victory in the elections of 2005, Yeltsin made a personal trip to Astana to attend the inauguration and share in the celebrations.

Among Nazarbayev's other friends were former US President George Bush Senior, King Juan Carlos I of Spain, the Russian leaders Putin and Dmitry Medvedev, the French President Nicolas Sarkozy.

The logical conclusion and theoretical development of the reforms that had already unfolded in Kazakhstan were to be found in the pioneering document 'Kazakhstan-2030', which identified new targets to be met by that year. 'I took the decision to develop a long-term strategy at the end of 1995,' Nazarbayev later recalled in his book *The Kazakhstan Way*. 'The fifth year of Kazakh independence had begun, and by then the reforms we had implemented had given us hope of stabilizing the economy. At the start of 1996, for the first time in the history of independent Kazakhstan, the economy showed a growth in GDP, at the small but promising rate of 0.5 per cent. We had vast oil reserves that would last us for thirty to forty years, and the concentration of foreign investors in Kazakhstan's Caspian Sea territory meant that the country's revenues were growing from year to year. The period of 'fire-fighting' was over, and we had more time to stop and think about what our country might achieve in ten, twenty or thirty years. Moreover, if you look at other countries that have successfully overcome crisis periods in their development, they have one thing in common: they meticulously planned the direction they were moving in, clearly allocated their resources, objectively assessed their strengths and weaknesses, and made clear their end goal.'

Famous programmes such as Roosevelt's 'New Deal', which allowed the US to escape the economic depression of the 1920s and 30s, Malaysia's 'Vision for 2020', and various strategic plans in China and South Korea, among others, were taken as examples. But Kazakhstan's Strategy, as Nazarbayev saw it, differed from theirs in that it was not confined solely to economic issues, but was a rather more complex document, a kind of 'road map' with which to address the priority issues in the country's development.

Practical work on the Strategy began in the summer of 1997. Nazarbayev, experienced in the preparation of important state documents, did not limit himself to merely supervising the project but took an active role in the creative process. The Agency for Strategic Planning, tasked with the development of this document, reported back to the President once every two weeks with newly completed versions incorporating the alterations and suggestions he had put forward. Around himself he assembled a large group of international specialists, which included such renowned experts as H. Berstok, K. Grey, V. Hudzhong, G. Allison, R. Blekvill among others.

Finally, by the autumn of 1997, the many months of hard work on the Strategy were over. In October Nazarbayev announced 'Kazakhstan-2030, for the prosperity, security and ever-growing welfare of every Kazakhstani. The Kazakhstan-2030 programme is my vision for the future of our society and the mission of our country. This is not dogma, nor a law which everyone is strictly obliged to follow. But to live without a purpose makes life itself meaningless. Therefore, Kazakhstan-2030 can become the vision of the future which guides our life. Our general goal is to build an independent, prosperous and politically stable Kazakhstan with a liberal outlook, national unity, strong democratic institutions, and social justice and economic well-being for the entire population.'

The Strategy contained seven key priorities: national security; political stability and consolidation of society; economic growth based on an open market economy with high levels of foreign investment and

The newly re-elected President arrives in Astana to be greeted by a guard of honour.

domestic savings; the health, education and welfare of the citizens of Kazakhstan; energy resources; infrastructure, transport and communications; and a professionally run state.

The Strategy identified a national goal and a system of long-term priorities for achieving it. Their realization was anticipated in the annual three- and five-year plans. Initially, many were warily of the Strategy, wondering whether the President might be looking too far ahead. But the logic was clear in the very text of the Strategy: 'I think that each one of us has come to understand that it is not possible to live only for today if you want to solve the problems of the age ... Having correctly identified our priorities and the means of achieving them, and shown the will and patience to follow this path, we must stop ourselves from veering off it, and wasting our effort, time and resources ... The difficult conditions in which we find ourselves today should not deprive us of energy and hope. A clear understanding of our ambitions and an honest explanation of the difficulties and dangers in the way can help mobilize all citizens towards this common goal.'

As for why the Strategy was based on a thirty-year period, it was roughly equivalent to the active adult life of a generation that might embrace these long-term objectives and their personal responsibility to meet them, and then enjoy the results of their efforts. The ultimate goal was the practical implementation of the Strategy into people's lives. From 1998 onwards, the government began to develop and introduce three-year strategic plans. Introduced on this basis were the Strategy of Industrial and Innovation Development, the State Agricultural Programme, the Rural Territories Development Programme, health, education and social security system reforms, Madeni Mura (Cultural Legacy), improved housing construction, and so on.

For Kazakhstan-2030 to work, further democratization of the political system was urgently required. To this end, in October 1998 the President initiated amendments and additions to the country's Constitution, which he announced in his Address to the Nation on 30 September 1998 entitled 'On Our Country's Situation and the Fundamental Direction of its Domestic and Foreign Policy: Democratization of Society, and Economic and Political Reform in the New Century'. He identified seven priorities for political liberalization. These included: improving the electoral system, ensuring that elections were free and just, strengthening the role of political parties, expanding the powers of Parliament, the development of civil society, the freedom of the press, an independent judiciary system and the improved status of women in society. However, the constitutional amendments proposed by the President were rejected by his MPs, and a series of counter-proposals were put forward, which addressed the strengthening of Parliamentary control over the use of the budget, the possibility of *akims* being elected in stages, and lengthened periods of activity for both of its chambers.

After some heated debates, on 7 October 1998 Parliament adopted the law 'On the Introduction of Amendments and Additions to the Constitution of the Republic of Kazakhstan', which consisted of nineteen changes. In particular, Parliament's power to control the government was increased; cities would be able to elect their own *akims*; a jury system was established; the presidential term was increased from five years to seven years, the term of Majilis deputies to five years, and that of members of the Senate to six years; a mixed majority-proportional electoral system was incorporated into the Majilis; ten seats were allotted for political parties to vote in someone from their party by proportional representation (limited to members of political parties who received more than 7 per cent of the vote), and so on.

In an address to MPs after the results of the voting were announced, Nazarbayev said: 'There has been many a dramatic moment over the past seven days. These seven days have, if not shocked, then at least stirred

The President swears allegiance to the nation of Kazakhstan.

Kazakhstan, and have not been easy for me. If I am honest, I had expected Parliament to support me on such important initiatives … To avoid a full-on confrontation, we created a conciliation commission and adopted a final version of the bill, which was voted on. I am grateful to Parliament for the compromise. I would like it to be noted that Kazakhstan managed to liberalize its political system in a difficult environment, especially given the global economic crisis. However, this is further evidence of the safety margin that we have created over the years.'

The amendments made to the Constitution raised the question of the timing of the presidential and parliamentary elections. In this instance, the President made the decision not to wait for the end of his term of office in 2000, but to go to the polls. On 22 October 1998 Nazarbayev sent out a statement announcing his decision to run as a Presidential candidate in the upcoming elections.

The presidential elections held on 10 January 1999 were, for the first time in the history of independent Kazakhstan, conducted on a competitive basis, this being one of the first practical steps to take effect from the constitutional reform of 1998. In this election, Nazarbayev won a landslide victory, with 79.78 per cent of the vote in support of him.

9

The Spirit
of Astana

A separate, personal page in the life of President Nursultan Nazarbayev and in the life of the nation was his epochal decision to move the capital, a deed which would become his *opus magnum* – one of the most important acts of his life.

Years later the switching of the Kazakh capital from Almaty to Akmola (today's Astana) would be called the most successful national project of independent Kazakhstan and the founding and evolution would be written in golden letters in world history. But at the very beginning it was not like this.

When the idea was first given voice by Nazarbayev in 1994 from the platform of the Supreme Union, society's reaction was ambivalent, if not to say negative. There was misunderstanding and doubt about the expedience and timeliness of such a step.

The new capital took shape from the precision of a street-by-street model.

But the idea had not been casually conceived. The history of Kazakhstan was such that, even regarding such a burning question as moving the capital, in the twentieth century Kazakhstan had been deprived of its own say in the matter. Orenburg, Kyzylorda and Almaty, each designated as capitals in the context of colonial and totalitarian dependence. Such designations did not reflect national self-determination.

As yet there were no precise calculations in construction or building costs. Hitherto opportunism may have prevailed over strategy, and indifference towards actual interests of the Republic had so far characterized the choice of sites for the capital. This led to a mass of problems, hindering the long-term development of such cities as capitals, and most importantly being unconducive for the balanced evolution of the country's regions. Thanks to all this there was a systemic failure in Almaty's territorial growth. It was limited by the mountains that enclosed the city, and a risk of earthquakes. In fairness it is worth noting that at the end of the 1920s, when it was decided to move capital from Kyzylorda, the new administrative centre of the Republic was to be built 'with a clean page', 120 kilometres north from Almaty, on the flatlands on the banks of the River Ili, but these plans were quickly and unashamedly abandoned.

In the summer of 1994 Nursultan Nazarbayev proposes to the Supreme Council initiatives on moving the capital.

Above:
The new parliamentary building is opened with due ceremony.

Below:
'I know the city shall come to be.' Nursultan Nazarbayev consults on the plans for the new capital.

Nazarbayev spoke as Head of the Republic when the change of capital was announced. Almaty was not capable, by economic or geopolitical conditions, of meeting the requirements of a capital of an independent state. With the population approaching 1.5 million, the city was becoming limited in the terms of the allocation of space. It was necessary to increase the size of Almaty's city-space, but due to an already high density of building and a lack of space in the urban territory, there was nowhere to expand. Moreover, there was high seismic risk in Almaty. The President noted that it would be significantly more expensive to build here in comparison with other Kazakh towns. Finally, the sovereign state of Kazakhstan desperately needed new administrative buildings. Hitherto there had been no need for a Parliament, a Ministry of Foreign Affairs, a Ministry of Defence, banks or embassies of foreign states. From year to year the ecological situation of Almaty worsened. The inescapable conclusion for Nazarbayev was that, as a capital, Almaty had disadvantages impossible to overcome.

City planners were given the authority to initiate a study of all the territories of the Republic with the aim of finding an optimal location for the new capital. It had to meet thirty-two parameters. The most important were social-economic factors, climate, landscape, seismic risk, surrounding environment, engineering and transport infrastructure, and finally, construction and labour resources. The analysis showed that from all the options, the most suitable was Akmola, which was near the geographical centre of Kazakhstan, close to important economic regions and in reach of transport links. And not insignificantly, already with a population of 300,000, it had the potential of naturally expanding its citizenry and living space without harming the environment.

The advantages of Akmola were in many senses linked with its position in the structure of the national economy as a capital of the Virgin Territories (Altai Territory), which had historical resonance from the 1950s and the exploration of its 'virgin' soil.

At the start of the 1950s the destruction of war and the unsuccessful implementation of village agriculture in the Soviet Union meant the country was incapable of satisfying the growing demand of an expanding population, even for basic food like bread, meat, milk, eggs and vegetables. Especially severe was the shortage of bread.

In March 1954, at the Plenary Session of the Central Committee of the CPSU, a decision was made to increase cultivated grain fields at the expense of exploiting fallow lands in the northern regions of Kazakhstan, Siberia, the Volga, the Urals, the Far East and the North Caucasus. The USSR state plan was to put no less than 43 million hectares to the plough countrywide.

The reclamation of virgin lands was done at a forced pace. By August 1954, 6.5 million hectares had already been ploughed in Kazakhstan. The following year, 9.4 million hectares were ploughed up. In 1956 the sum total of newly cultivated land reached 20 million hectares, three times more than planned. From 1954 to 1960, 25.5 million hectares were ploughed, or 61 per cent of all plots of new land in USSR, which were organized into some 600 collective farms, increasing the quantity of state farms and smallholdings several times over. One result was the waste of massive financial resources from both Union and Republic budgets.

The first years of the reclamation of virgin lands were successful enough. Although there was a lack of crucial infrastructure – roads, grain stores, living spaces, repair centres for state farms – for a brief period Kazakhstan became an important grain provider for the USSR. In 1956 the Republic had already given the country one billion poods (16 kilograms) of grain, and in the best years provided 100 to 110 million poods. Overall, a record harvest was taken in the country of 125 million tonnes of grain, of which 50 per cent was from virgin soil.

The previous town of Akmola was to develop at speed.

But the reclamation of virgin lands had a range of negative consequences. Ignorance of the specific requirements of virgin soil, relating to soil erosion and moisture content, led to frequent dust storms, and to the loss of fruitful soil. Tillage depleted from 25.5 million hectares of virgin earth, the crop-producing power of 9 million hectares was completely lost and removed from economic turnover. From the start of the 1960s began the frequent occurrence of drought. The effectiveness of virgin soil fell each year. In 1965 wind erosion affected not only Kazakh land, but the Altai border, Bashkiria, Kalmykia, the Volga and other areas of Russia. The degradation of soil threatened to become irreversible and to lead to catastrophe.

A rational agricultural planning system for virgin lands only came to be implemented almost two decades after the start of blanket

reclamation. It was developed by the director of the All-Union Institute of Grain Economy A.I. Barayev, and his colleagues.

The basis of the soil protection system consisted in such methods as crop rotation, the subsoil enrichment, exploiting optimal periods for sowing and seeding, a change to phosphor fertilization to speed up crop maturation and the quality of grain, a change of herbicide and pre-harvest appraisal of the quality of grain. By 1975, this had taken place on 12 million hectares, and over a period of ten years the Republic completely moved across to this new system.

Capital Day is celebrated with pageantry.

The ploughing of giant plots of virgin earth led to a severe shortage in Kazakhstan of haymaking and pasture, and wrought huge damage in a traditional branch of village agriculture in the Republic – cattle breeding. The meat and dairy industries declined.

The mass migration of workers into Kazakhstan from the RSFSR (Russian Socialist Federative Socialist Republic), Ukraine, Belarus and Moldova, reached 2.5 million. By 1962 Kazakhs accounted for less than a third of the population of the Republic – no more than 29 per cent in total. Thus a real threat had emerged to the language, socio-cultural institutions and to the protection of the Kazakh ethnicity in general.

Today, there exist various opinions on this expediency in the reclamation of virgin and fallow lands, ranging from slight disagreements to diametrical opposition. But for all the disparity of view, a wide-angle assessment is valuable. The disadvantages and miscalculations should not mask the sense of achievement and the advantages Kazakhstan still enjoys, thanks to the virgin lands: the Republic not only provided its own grain, but had become one of the ten leading exporters of grain in the world, and a provider of food for countries in need.

Spaciousness and grace
characterize the heart
of the new capital.

The move to a new capital may be seen as a strategic response to global cries for help, which had arisen in a period where initiating independence was proving complex. It was no coincidence that a move to a new capital chimed with the unveiling of the 'Kazakhstan-2030' Strategy.

Patriot and warrior Kenesary Khan kept alive Kazakh identity as Russian colonialism spread in past times.

It was an extremely testing time for the young state, quite literally fighting for its survival, struggling out of a deep and protracted economic and political crisis with everyone pulling their weight.

A no less alarming situation was taking shape in the global economy, with the thunderclouds of a financial crisis in Southwest Asia and a market crash in Russia gathering. Despite all this, not a single country of the former USSR hesitated to make the crucial move to responsibility for its own affairs.

Khan Shatyr Entertainment Centre: Astana's futuristic tent-shaped shopping mall and leisure site.

Iconic new buildings of grace dominate the skyline of today's Astana.

Thus, the Supreme Union to which the President was answerable, issued a decree 'Regarding the Change of Capital of the Republic of Kazakhstan', which in effect bowed to Nazarbayev's authority. In the ensuing period of the USSR's collapse and the start of the cruellest of crises, this served to safeguard the Republic from the flames of interethnic and inter-citizen hostility, to bulwark political stability and chart a route between various obstacles and pitfalls, patiently building up a means for the modernization of the country.

The public disclosure of this decision at home and abroad saw the mass media by and large responding negatively, albeit reflecting the mood of society. Therefore, throughout the following years, down to the unveiling of the new capital itself, Nursultan Nazarbayev was forced to defend the expediency of his proposal. 'The decision to change the political centre of the country to the city of Astana was not reactionary or capriciously made by the will of one man or a few. This was a deeply considered, historically justified, forward-thinking decision, taken with the aim of enriching lives across the nation,' Nazarbayev explained. 'The new century places new challenges before us. We have to create a new state. Kazakhstan is a Eurasian country, and in our move to the centre of the state there is a reflection of the many-sided orientation of our foreign policy, and what integration means to us. To set up amicable mutual relations with the entire world, to be a thoughtful and open neighbour – such is our aim.' This was Nazarbayev's persistent theme in his meetings with the people.

The Head of State gave full expression to the reasons for changing capitals in his book *In the Heart of Eurasia*.

At the same time the President oversaw the strict implementation of the decision. In 1995, the State Commission was formed through the relocation of the higher and central organs of government to Akmola. Between 1995 and 1997, a range of important decrees and regulations were issued, focused on the development of Akmola. Requirements for the new capital included the creation of the Akmola Special Economic Zone as well as the extra-budgetary fund for the new capital and the creation of the Eurasian University of L.N. Gumilev, besides others. Thus a firm economic and legal base was formed for stimulating local and foreign investment, providing a system of taxation and trade in luxury goods.

The head of government personally oversaw all matters on the subject linked to the approaching move. He visited Akmola on more than one occasion to oversee the ceremonial transfer of objects of state symbolism from Almaty to Akmola, and to raise the flag of Kazakhstan in the future capital.

The change of capital was achieved at record speed. This was extremely important to foster optimism among Kazakhs in this period of crisis. It became a significant event, a meaningful transition for the country from past to future.

On 10 December 1997, the President, Parliament and government settled down to work in their new capital. Nazarbayev said: 'Today we, the highest bodies of authority of the Republic of Kazakhstan, triumphantly announce that from 10 December 1997 Akmola is the capital of our state. From now on and for the foreseeable future we will make decisions in the centre of this huge country, in a momentous move

A gift from Russia, the Triumph of Astana office building and hotel, soars to 142 metres.

for the nation. The heart of our homeland now beats here. From here Kazakhstan will define its historical destiny at the threshold of a third millennium ... we will be content with this choice!' With this exhortation he spoke to the nation.

After half a year, the international unveiling of the new capital took place. Literally on the eve of this important event, it gained a new name. Since the name of the city – Akmola – was historically based, it was

'Memories of faithful ancestors' – at the opening of Astana's memorial for victims of political oppression.

Astana's Palace of Peace and Accord is 77 metres tall.

construed differently and yielded ambivalent responses amongst society, and the question of the expediency of renaming the capital arose.

The press broke into stormy debate, with writers, philologists and historians taking part. Various names were put forward – Karaotkel, Yesil, Ishim, Saryarka, Kazakhstan and even Nursultan. The President attentively followed these debates. In his opinion, the name of the capital should have a clear connotation, in connection with which he proposed the idea that the capital be called Astana, as the Kazakh term for 'capital'. On 6 May 1998, the President's decree was released, 'Regarding the Renaming of the Town of Akmola to Astana'.

In those days, the city resembled a restless ant colony. With the aim of speeding the work, many were working a triple-shift regime. The President did not make exception for himself. Having worked all day, he would call meetings in the middle of the night. Step-by-step, with schematics, graphics, maps and tables he planned the entire organization of the unveiling of the city, beginning from entry into the town and ending in the escorting of departing guests. Under the gimlet gaze of the Head of State no detail was overlooked: the preparation of the airport and train station, the planning of travel destinations, the arrangement of the banks of the Yesil and the planting of greenery, the layout and lighting of streets, the reconstruction of the Hall of Congress, the setting up of a university, stadium and hotels, listing invited artists and stages of theatrical performances, the sale of books and souvenirs, the draining of the swamp ... and during these long hours, when it seemed there was nothing to laugh about, he always found a way to calm the atmosphere and heighten people's mood with a joke or witty anecdote.

At the unveiling of the capital on 10 June 1998, the President of Turkey S. Demirel, the Azerbaijani President H.A. Aliyev, the Uzbek President I.A. Karimov, and the Kyrgyzstani President A.A. Akayev were present. Among the honorary guests of Astana were the Prime Minister of Tajikistan Y.N. Asimov, the Prime Minister of Armenia A.P. Darbinyan, the Deputy Prime Minister of Belarus G.V. Novitsky, the secretaries general of the Organization of the Islamic Conference A. Laraki and of the Organization of Economic Cooperation O. Ozar.

An impressive Russian delegation arrived, headed by the plenipotentiary representative of the President of the Russian Federation in the CIS, I.P. Rybkin. Amongst the delegation was the President of the Republic of Tatarstan M. S. Shameyev, the President of the Republic of Sakha (Yakutia) M.E. Nikolayev, the Governor of the Kemerovo region A.G. Tuleyev, and representatives of the mayors of the cities of Moscow and St Petersburg.

The unveiling was covered by some 300 journalists, representing the mass media of all leading countries.

At the ceremonial gathering the first amongst the guests to speak was the Turkish leader S. Demirel, who fulsomely praised Kazakhstan's success as a state, as it confidently strode ahead of the modern world. Congratulations followed from I.A. Karimov underlining, 'the courage of Nursultan Nazarbayev, taking responsibility upon himself for the change of capital' and expressing confidence that future generations would appreciate this with gratitude. The President of Ukraine, L.D. Kuchma, described Nursultan Nazarbayev's choice as 'correct'. G.A. Aliyev reminded attendees that, 'once Kazakhstan was deprived of the right to determine the location of its own capital'. The repositioning of its administrative centre to Astana was, 'the most productive move since Kazakhstan has gained independence'. The President of Kyrgyzstan memorably described Astana as 'the Eurasian Palmyra', and 'a sacred place in the great plains'.

Astana became not only politically and economically, but in its very personality, a personal project of Nazarbayev. In 2003, in answer to the

The 97-metre high Baiterek Tower was to become Astana's most famous landmark, a symbol of the holy tree in which the mythological bird Samruk laid its shining eggs. It is flanked by administrative buildings.

question of whether the President personally took part in the planning and building of the capital, he responded to the *Wall Street Journal*: 'Each and every home. Each architectural project. It seemed even the light of each house ... I am an architect and am not ashamed to say it.'

Immediately after the move to the capital in Akmola, at the start of its reconstruction and modernization to the plans of Nazarbayev, there was erected the monument to the defenders of the motherland 'Otan

Ana' and the presidential centre of culture. The idea for the other monument 'Astana-Baiterek', which would become a tourist attraction of the capital comparable to Paris's Eiffel Tower or the Statue of Liberty in New York, is also ascribable to the President. Behind it lay the old Kazakh legend of the magical bird Samruk, which each year laid a golden egg in the crown of the Mogucheva Monument, bringing life and hope.

For the long-term development of the capital, Nazarbayev proposed an international competition for a general plan in accord with modern architectural ideas. Architects from Europe, Asia, America and Australia took part as well as an artistic team from the CIS countries and Kazakhstan. The winner, the Japanese architect K. Kurokawa, began a world famous project which envisaged the erection of the new administrative centre on the left bank of the river Yesil as the core of the capital.

The characteristic feature of Astana, which everyone came to notice, is in the surprisingly multifaceted building style, underlining the city's status as a modern Eurasian capital, whereby progressive architectural solutions are seen comfortably alongside traditional values of steppe culture.

The first pearls of the town became the President's residence 'Akorda', the Palace of Peace and Accord, the House of Ministries, the Parliament building and the state company 'KazMunaiGas', a green seaside boulevard with the Astana-Baiterek Monument soaring nearby, the round plaza and the singing fountains on the bank of the river Yesil, the Atameken Ethnopark, the Kazakh Eli Monument, the triumphal arch, an aquarium, the Nur Astana Mosque, the Cathedral of the Holy Assumption, the Kazakhstan central concert hall, an ultramodern media centre, a spacious schoolchildren's play area, magnificent five-star hotels Rixos, Beijing Palace and Ramada Plaza Astana, the shopping entertainment centre Khan Shatyr, Keruen Cinema Park and Mega Centre; the business centres Astana Tauer, Moscow Park, St Petersburg, and the most beautiful living accommodation, Triumph of Astana, the Emerald Quarter, On the Water-green Boulevard, Northern Lights, Highvill, Grand Alatau and several others.

Many unique structures were planned, such as the largest grand mosque in central Asia, Hazret Sultan, a grandiose eighty-eight-storey administrative-living complex, Abu-Dhabi Plaza, new opera and ballet theatres, a book archive and the Library of the First President amongst other buildings.

'I built this city,' remarked the President.

Such experienced masters as the British architect Norman Foster, who was behind the shopping and entertainment complex Khan Shatyr – one of the tallest and most original buildings in tent-shaped form in the world – and the Palace of Peace and Accord – designed in the image of the pyramids – set to work on the creation of this uniquely stylish capital, along with the Italian architect Nicoletti, who designed the Kazakhstan central concert hall.

A separate page in the architectural history of the capital was connected to the arrival of the seventh Winter Asian Games, taking

place in Kazakhstan in January–February 2011, a memorable event in the life of the country. For their opening, a range of sports buildings were constructed, including the Alau indoor skating stadium and the Republic's cycling track, Saryarka. A little earlier an indoor football stadium, Astana-Arena, had appeared in the city with a retractable roof and 30,000 seats.

Speaking at the celebratory ceremony of the opening of the games, the Head of State noted with pride that Kazakhstan had become the first amongst the CIS countries and in the entire Muslim world to lead

President Nazarbayev and the invited heads of foreign governments at the opening of the seventh Winter Asian Games, taking place in Astana and Almaty.

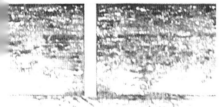

such a continental forum. The Winter Asian Games, he stressed, were the second largest competition after the Olympics, and up to then only three countries had been economically advanced enough to host the games: Japan, China and South Korea. Now Kazakhstan could be counted in this number.

As a whole, with its attainment of independence the evolution of physical education and sport in Kazakhstan reached a new level. Thanks to the constant stewardship of the President and government support of physical education and sport, Kazakh sportsmen joined the elite of Asia. Many of them won events at the Olympic Games and other championships in the world. In national programmes, many sports federations, clubs, schools and classes were opened in the country, stimulating tourism and recreational facilities. Each year new sports complexes, fitness centres, swimming pools and stadiums were built, without comparison in the world. Many were built to revive national games, such as Kazaksha Kures, Kokpar, Baige, Audaryspak, Asyk, Kryz Kuu, Zharys and Togyz-Kumalak.

The Head of State's commitment to the health of the nation lay behind all of this. He has stressed, 'It is very important to introduce the cult of a healthy way of living into the everyday lives and consciousnesses of each family, each person, and especially the youth, in the most decisive way. This is a strategic priority, as the future of a country directly depends on setting up a healthy nation.'

The President is an active example of a healthy way of life. Sport occupies an honoured position. Acquainting himself with sport in early childhood, even at a mature age Nursultan Nazarbayev took up tennis, acquainted himself with golf and, at sixty, mastered mountain climbing. Mastering sports, for him, is not so much entertainment as a citizen's duty. The Head of State's physical fitness is a requirement, not simply for his own sake but in the cause of the effective functioning of state leadership. Namely, his love of sports and systematic self-discipline allow him to work actively and productively, helping to take the strain of heavy physical and mental demands.

The Kazakh capital can boast yet more than modern administrative, cultural and leisure and sports centres. In the city, leading scientific and educational centres of the Republic are developing rapidly in the form of the Nazarbayev University and the Eurasian National University, where a modern medical unit is being created with six specialized health divisions. An industrial park provided the infrastructure for hi-tech innovation.

The new capital has turned into a genuinely green oasis, with spacious parks and numerous congenial squares. This is largely due to the work of Nazarbayev. Alongside the creation of parks more than 50,000 hectares were allocated for woodlands. This manmade forest, where a variety of animal and birds settled, was to spread northwards and join with the extensive forest at the Shuchinsko-Borovsky resort.

In a short period Astana attained not only the lustre appropriate for a capital city, it had become a real political, economic and cultural centre for the country, having its own individual personality and ambience.

Today Astana reflects the thrust of the whole country, as a locomotive for political and economic advances. The attraction of Astana with its potential for long-term growth is reflected by the huge financial resources of local and foreign investors. The momentum behind the building and development of the capital gathers pace with each year.

Following the example of Astana, other cities of the country are developing likewise.

Time has justified the President's decision. Even the most convinced sceptics have acknowledged not only the historical necessity, but the political and economic expedience of Nazarbayev's initiative. The change of capital opened a new epoch in Kazakh history – an epoch released from the influence of the past. It became a symbol of the economic growth of the country, the spiritual growth of the nation and the blossoming of society.

The story of the transfer of capital is characterized by the leader's formula of reform: an innovative plan produced a result that impressed all, with a smooth integration into habitual life, and the period between conception and realization, minimal.

Nazarbayev opens the
capital's surrounding forest
of imported plants.

10

Kazakhstan – The Only Way is Forward

At his official enrolment as President of the Republic of Kazakhstan, on 20 January 1999, Nursultan Nazarbayev repeated his devotion to his chosen commitment. 'In politics it is a rare thing to remember a period when it can be said that a day outlasts a century; 10 January 1999 became such a day for our country and for myself. In Kazakhstan that date became a watershed, a dividing line between the bloody and dramatic twentieth century and the hopeful and expectant twenty-first.

The people rally in support of the leadership in a spirit of unity.

'Today before me stand two simple tasks. But history teaches us that they are the most complicated. As a rule, our ancestors' highest praise could be summed up thus: "They fed their people well". The first requirement, therefore, is the wellbeing of the nation. There is time to throw stones, and there is time to collect stones. There is time to push through reforms, and there is time to harvest fruit from reforms. For the next seven years, the nation should see the fruits of reforms on its table and in its pocket.

'The second task is the development of democracy in the country. By a newly made law, we will have an election this year for Parliament. All political parties can take part in this battle during the forty-nine weeks until the new millennium. There is no alternative to freedom.

'I have just taken the oath of the President of the Republic of Kazakhstan. I swore to observe our constitution, our laws, our national honour and our dignity. And I will never break this promise. Gathering strength from our sacred past, we will steadfastly go forward to meet the new century!'

Responding to the challenges confronting him the President defined the range of his roles for the democratization of society. On the political agenda was the decentralization of government control, the expansion of the electoral register, the liberalization of electoral rules, heightening the authority of representative organs of government, and the strengthening of civil society as represented by the party, NGOS and the media.

Decentralizing state control called for the demarcation of the lines between various layers of power, and the enhancement of inter-governmental relations. The President created a State Commission for the decentralization of government functions and intergovernmental relations and ordered the preparation of a suitable solution. This work was completed in February 2003.

In 2001, a programme for the election of local leaders was begun. A central aim was to empower such people and so bring any given local area to fully engage with its own problems and the care of its inhabitants.

The idea of making *akims* eligible to run for power had been announced by the Head of State in 1998. That year the first steps were taken. On a trial basis, local *akim* elections were held in the village of Shamalgan, in the Karasai district of the Almaty region. In October 2001, the pilot project expanded to include twenty-eight village cantons (two districts per region).

Opposite:
'Democracy is our choice; democracy is our fate.'

Within the framework of mutual cooperation with the institutes of Civil Society, a range of steps were taken in relation to political parties, NGOs and mass media.

The participation of parties in parliamentary elections was to be governed by proportional representation. With elections taking place on 10 October 1999, ten places were allocated for division among the Otan, Citizens, Agrarian and Communist parties.

Nazarbayev gave his State of the Nation address on the eve of the elections: 'Elections in the Majilis and *maslikhat* [local representative bodies] demonstrate the success of our efforts in encouraging an increase in the amount of political parties. Nine parties will contest for space in the new Majilis in the electoral districts and party list. They represent their own vision of the future of our country, exposed to all on national television. A total of 559 candidates will contest for sixty-seven single-member places in the Majilis, averaging eight candidates per place. More than 7000 candidates will fight for a place in the *maslikhat*. The Kazakh citizen will have a wide choice when it comes to filling out his electoral ballot paper this Sunday ... I urge you to make sure that 10 October will be written in our annals as the day on which multiparty democracy was born in the Republic of Kazakhstan'.

In 2002, on the President's initiative, a lively council was set up for promoting suggestions for the long-term democratization and evolution of Civil Society. The council's first act was creating a mechanism for dialogue on the coordination of the key administrative processes, involving the institutes of Civil Society.

A new law was made 'Regarding Political Parties', aimed at strengthening the party system by creating strong parties, using structures from different layers of the population. The logic behind the plan for the country's development constantly demanded that, alongside strengthening the state, political parties grew and were strengthened, leading to the political and civil self-expression.

The Otan Party emerged pre-eminent, formed out of three reformists' parties – the Party of National Unity of Kazakhstan, the Democratic Party of Kazakhstan, and the Socialist Movement of Kazakhstan. Vigorous growth was seen among NGOs, which grew to number almost five thousand.

This period was also marked by the increase in the role of the media. In March 2002, Nazarbayev took part in the first Congress of Journalists of Kazakhstan. One of the significant results of the congress was the creation of the Public Council for Media under the President of the country. At the council, questions were posed on the activity of the President in the formation of policy on the transparency of information, on public relations in the field of mass media, on the defence of lawful rights of the media, on state involvement in media issues and other situations of dispute in the sphere of mass media.

Thus guaranteeing rights and freedoms of citizens was enhanced. In September 2002, the institute of the Commissioner for Human Rights (Ombudsman) was set up.

In 2004, the process of liberalizing the political system, within the framework of the 1998 constitution, received a boost. Nazarbayev's message 'For the Competitiveness of Kazakhstan, the Competitiveness of Society of Economy, the Competitiveness of the Nation', was used on 19 March. It spoke of the need for the extension of democratic reforms as one of the key conditions for ensuring the country's competitiveness.

The argument of his message was published in the 'National Programme of Political Reform', released on 7 June by the extraordinary session of the Otan Party.

Guidelines for decentralizing government were specified: liberalization of electoral lawmaking; the gradual introduction of the eligibility of *akims* in government; the widening of the powers of Parliament, especially on the basis of a parliamentary majority; the completion of a system of state services; the strengthening of mutual cooperation with institutes of civil society; and toughening of the eradication of corruption.

The Head of State called on the public to take part in the all-inclusive discussion announced to them in the programmes of political reforms. Platforms for dialogue were created through vigorous consultation, long-term democratization, a National Commission for Democracy and Civil Society under the President and, lastly, the National Commission for Development and Concretization of Democratic Reforms. The results of this national discussion were laid out in the constitutional reforms of 2007.

In the development of a breakout of nationwide discussion about the mediums of democratization in the country through the initiative of Nazarbayev, specialized platforms for dialogue were also formed and developed, the most powerful of which was the Public Council for Media and the Citizens' Forum.

And so, on 31 March 2003, under the Head of State, the first meeting of the Public Council for Media took place. 'The creation of a

Public Council for Media is a new step towards the press mastering its role and demonstrating itself as an equal partner in the resolution of problems and challenges of the country,' Nazarbayev said at the start of the first meeting. 'The Council should become a consolidating structure which, taking its creation as a sign of its own empowerment, will help the press, state and society in the aim of sustaining mutual understanding, as well as the norms and laws on which the country was set up. Only on this basis will we be able to guarantee the protection of democratic principles in the sphere of mass media. Democracy and freedom are not possible without a strict observance of lawfulness.'

Of the non-governmental sector Nazarbayev said, opening the Civil Forum on 15 October 2003, 'We are talking about the formation of a new model for a relationship in which the government and NGOs will act as partners. It is therefore important to define a strategy for cooperation. We have a shared aim – to ensure the stable advance in the direction of liberalism, to build up the state's economic strength, the juristic function of the state and to encourage the evolution of Civil Society. Our forum should provide a veritable thrust in this direction, and provide suggestions for long-term cooperation.'

The state programme Madeni Mura ('Cultural Heritage') became the most important event in the cultural life of the country, the idea behind which the Head of State spoke of in his message to the nation on 4 April 2003. It should complete the next tasks; namely to create a focused system of education based on the rich cultural heritage of the nation, including modern national culture, folklore, traditions and customs; and to ensure the erection of significant historical-cultural and architectural monuments, having a special focus on national history; it should incorporate the experience of many centuries of national literature and authorship and create an extended artistic, scientific, and biographical educational curriculum; lastly it should create in the State language a fully-fledged fund for education in the humanities based on the best international scientific, cultural and literary precepts.

At the tenth session of the National Assembly, Nazarbayev said: 'We are talking not about the birth of a form of political behaviour, but about the treasures of our ancient and modern culture which give us moral strength, and help us to hold ourselves together in the swirl of history. Sometimes history corresponds with the adage, "What sons forget, grandsons remember." The birth of culture is a shared affair. The cultural heritage of Kazakhstan includes not only Kazakh culture, but the culture of each ethnicity living in our country. Therefore national-

The first Civil Forum took place in Astana on 15 October 2003.

cultural centres should actively participate in the realization of this programme.'

Reforms no less important were occurring in the economic sphere, first of all protecting Kazakhstan from the effects of the Asian financial crisis of 1997–98, breaking out in the countries of the south and east, and the market crash in Russia in 1998.

That financial crisis became the first serious test of national economic stability. The country held up manfully, demonstrating its self-reliance in a crisis situation. This was made possible by the economic reforms introduced by Nazarbayev.

Despite the situation, the President spelled out the building blocks of the reforms in health care, education, culture, communal-living households and the pension system.

These areas were the cause of the biggest dissatisfaction among the population. The laws of the market were the determining factor. By the end of the 1990s the government had been weakened; but the hardship was for necessary change. The provision of credit, pension reform, communal living households, education, and healthcare were all

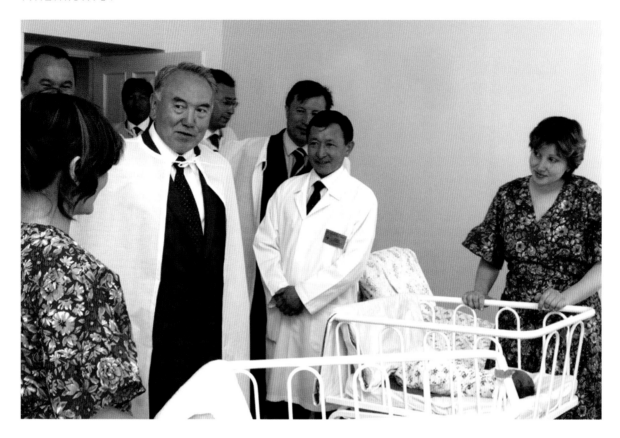

The health of mothers and infants: an example of the government's frontline healthcare.

addressed and tackled, while in the majority of neighbouring states these reforms remained precarious in the face of social unrest.

In this period, serious friction ensued between the state and the powerful local financial-industrial groups demanding a re-evaluation of certain aspects of the national economy, against the worsening international backdrop.

During this time the instinct of national 'oligarchs' was to hide behind a front of liberalism. Conflict spread from the economic to the political. An array of financial-industrial groups publically declared their disagreement with the 'authoritarian' course set by Nursultan Nazarbayev which they declared to be impeding long-term democratization. At root, there was an effort to blackmail those in power, under the guise of supporting the international community. After that failed they made a direct call for the radical transformation of the political system. Again, as in the mid 1990s, a real threat emerged that reforms would be dismantled. Nazarbayev stood against this conservative pro-communist faction, headed by what was then the Supreme Council.

Nazarbayev took the 'Oligarchs' Revolt' badly, since he himself had at one time 'by his own hand' brought many of them into business and into the system of government. At this worsening juncture the President adopted an intransigent stance against what he described as anti-Kazakh 'Oligarch capitalism'.

Governmental measures allowed Kazakhstan to escape the worst consequences of the economic crisis. By 1999, the country achieved a small but growing GDP – a level of 5.3 per cent growth. Industrial production grew by 0.5 per cent. Harvest of grain achieved a record 15.9 million tonnes (by comparison, in 1998 this was 7.5 million tonnes).

Notably, that same year, leading international rating agencies Standard & Poor's and Moody's gave Kazakhstan long-term credit ratings. In 2002 Kazakhstan was the first of the CSI countries to become an active market economy. All of this bore witness to the increase of faith in the potential of our economy.

The creation of the National Fund and the Stabilization Fund, initiated by Nazarbayev, was made possible by market realization of raw materials and instituted in order to protect the country from sudden crises and cataclysms.

Kazakhs see the fruits of reform on their tables.

The Head of State explained, 'We created a national fund in order to accumulate means of development for future generations. That is one side of the issue. The other – no less important – is to protect our people from crises and cataclysms. Remember, in 1997 we had no spare funds, nor indeed in 1996 or 1995. For months and years we could not pay for anything. Teachers and doctors did not receive payment, soldiers were not properly fed, towns stood still – times were hard. All of this we now thankfully forget. But we are still not fully impervious to such cataclysms.

'As ever we are focused on raw materials, and the prices of raw materials fluctuate. If tomorrow the price of oil rises or falls none shall be affected. If the exchequer loses a lot of money, will we go out into the world again with open arms? No.

'Any family tries to save for a rainy day, but the government, even more so. Therefore I created this fund, using our constitutional powers, which delegates the running of the nation of Kazakhstan to me. I have to think about Kazakhstan's tomorrow, and its day-after-tomorrow. It is for this that we are applying these methods.'

The President then spoke out strongly about the ill-thought-out suggestions for disseminating the fund's resources: 'Today I see a lively child, working in government, who does not make proper plans, and now suggests: "Let's spend this 2 billion on mothers with lots of children..." and so on. Such intelligence! They did not earn, or think about how to earn, this money and now come up with: "Let's spend..." Such thoughtless actions should be rejected by the nation. Such programmes are needed by no one and are harmful for Kazakhstan, absolutely harmful. We must spend our money rationally and according to precedent ... If this 2 billion is spent at a go, inflation will shoot up to heaven! Thus we will ruin our macroeconomic structure again. And so I express a certain disbelief at the initiatives of these so-called economists.'

Consequently, amid the fall-out from the world economic crisis in 2007, 10 billion dollars drawn from the National Fund essentially saved Kazakhstan and ensured the prosperity of its citizens, carrying it safely through the ruinous impact of uncontrollable economic chaos which had demolished a not-inconsiderable, age-old financial edifice, until then considered indestructible.

For Kazakhstan, 2003 became a watershed moment. It signified the defence and the completion of complex structural reforms of the 1990s, and the start of incremental economic growth. In 2003, it became

Children – the future
of our country.

evident that the crucial portion of the first decade of independence, including a change in socio-economic priorities, had been successful.

In terms of GDP per capita Kazakhstan shot up to second place amongst the CSI countries after Russia and, according to practically every socio-economic indicator, joined the world's economic leaders. An increase in production occurred across the board, showing the rate of inflation, steadying the tenge, and significantly increasing gold-cash reserves.

Kazakhstan's ascension to a new plane of socio-economic development allowed it to set about the essential modernization and diversification of the economy, with the aim of improving its competitiveness.

From 2003, the strategy for the industrial innovation development of Kazakhstan up to 2015 began. It aimed at escaping from an economy specializing in raw materials towards a rigorous development of scientific and hi-tech industries.

The strategy envisages the energy-output ratio of GDP falling by half between 2000 and 2015, and the role of scientific and hi-tech industries growing more than tenfold. The final aim of the programme was to direct Kazakhstan's evolution towards being a service-technical centre for the region, orientated towards hi-tech industry and services for neighbouring rapidly emerging economies.

To fulfil the strategy, a group of institutions for development were swiftly established. These included the Development Bank of Kazakhstan, the Investment and Innovation Fund, the Fund for the Development of Small Businesses, the Centre of Market and Analytic Research, the Corporation for the Insurance of Exports and Investments, and the Kazakh Centre for Assisting Investors – Kazinvest.

The priority then was to develop hi-tech industry. The government started to create a specialized techno-park – a centre of information technology in the town of Alatau below Almaty, a biotechnical centre in the city of Stepnogorsk in the Akmola region, and a centre of nuclear technology in the town of Kurchatov in the East Kazakhstan region. Taking the continued operation of the Baikonur Cosmodrome in Kazakhstan into account, it made sense to make a separate sphere for space technology.

In a message to the nation on 19 March 2004, entitled 'For a Competitive Kazakhstan, a Competitive Economy, and a Competitive Nation', the President said: 'It is extremely important to draw attention away from the temporary benefits of surrendering the lease of the Baikonur complex to the realization of cooperation with the Russian Space programme and projects ... This will aid the development of our space sciences and new technologies.'

A milestone for the Baikonur Cosmodrome was reached in 2005 when man's first space station of reached its fiftieth anniversary. It was a life-changing moment for the space business of Kazakhstan. On 25 January 2005, the President confirmed the State Programme of the Development of Space Activities for the years 2005–7. This programme opened a new chapter in the development of space affairs in Kazakhstan. From this moment, Kazakhstan set about constructing its own space industry.

It is apt to recall that before this success, a long and complex debate with Russia had been in train over the jurisdiction of the cosmodrome, and the related issue of support and implementation of joint space projects.

Meanwhile, Kazakhstan continued its quest to diversify means of exporting energy sources. And so, in May 2004, at the start of the state visit of the Head of China, an agreement was signed for the construction of the Atasu-Alashankou oil line. This was a real breakthrough, since up to then Kazakhstan's potential outlets were directed to or via Russia.

The Atasu-Alashankou pipeline came into operation in December 2005. It was the first long-distance Kazakhstan-China pipeline, uniting the Caspian oil field of Kazakhstan with China. With the fully complete construction of the Kazakhstan-China pipeline in 2009, the export of Kazakh oil to the East was assured. It was the centrepiece of a plan for the diversification of exports of Kazakh energy resources worldwide.

Remarkably, the industrial-innovation strategy proved its value in its first year of operation. By the end of 2003, five petrochemical enterprises had been renewed; the operation of zinc-producing factories at Balkhash was initiated, a polyethylene pipe in Atyrau was installed, a dock and infrastructure for supporting marine operations in the Caspian Sea were set up; the launch of the Kostanai diesel factory was announced; and the reconstruction and re-equipment of the entire range of light industry and foodstuffs was realized. In 2003, the rate of growth in converted industry outperformed the growth of other industries, surpassed only by the 20 per cent growth of the auto industry.

Concurrantly, the agrarian sector was reformed. The logic behind this economic metamorphosis required the modernization of village agriculture, and the formation of a rational structure of agricultural business, heightened competitiveness, and the evolution of a market strategy for farming and import substitution for the home market.

Nazarbayev always considered the development of the countryside, where more than 40 per cent of the population of the country live and work, as of prime importance. He constantly pointed out that 'if we do not raise the countryside up, we will not be able to raise the country up.' But saving the outdated and ineffective village farming system was one of the most complicated economic challenges before him. Despite the yearly injection of financial support, difficulties escalated year upon year. Dependence on the earth led to a fall in productivity and to the degeneration of the countryside.

Hence, the introduction of private ownership of agricultural land became a pressing issue. 'Only thus will we be able to create a

sustainable land economy, which will be protected so that we can pass it on to our children,' the President stressed.

Even despite the benefits of the reform, a serious dispute flared up around the matter. The Soviet mentality was again rearing its head, not able to accept that the land could have an owner other than the government. Debate on the Land Code project in 2003 caused a bitter standoff between government and Parliament. A stormy dispute between the lawmakers led to a lack of faith in government.

Considering the ambivalent relationship in society towards private ownership of land, the President took the matter into his own hands, patiently explaining the necessity of the decreed step through the pages of the press, speaking at countless meetings with the people and parliamentary deputies. Thus, on the eve of the parliamentary elections on the Land Code, the President took part in the meeting of both chambers in order to demonstrate to the lawmakers his position and to secure a compromise over the most hotly debated articles of the Land Code. In 2003, private ownership was finally introduced.

In Kazakhstan the livestock population is growing year upon year due to the new impetus behind the development of agriculture.

The countryside got a boost for its own self-actualized development. Within the framework of the State Agro-Food Programme in the years 2003–5 and the State Programme of the Development of Rural Territories of the Republic of Kazakhstan in 2004–10, for three consecutive years the government invested more than 150 billion tenge in the agrarian sector. Because of this, the Agro-Food Programme's development of rural territories was normalizing the attainability of creature comforts in villages, on the basis of the optimally efficient resettlement of the village population.

Nazarbayev considered the application of the land reforms as one of the most critical stages in the history of Kazakhstan and equated its significance and scope with that of general privatization. With the introduction of private ownership of land the period of transition in the economy was at an end, and Kazakhstan joined the group of market economy states.

In the international political arena, the start of a new millennium was marked by a raft of international initiatives for Kazakhstan, guaranteeing the country's entry to a new level of international validation and acknowledgement as a centre for running authoritative international forums. The prime exemplars of this were the First Conference on Interaction and Confidence Building Measures in Asia (CICA) and the First Congress of World and Traditional Religions. They had special resonance for the international community following the tragic event of 11 September 2001 in the USA, the worst terrorist act in modern history committed within the borders of that country.

These forums were not coincidental. Long before Nazarbayev had been repeatedly warning the international community about the danger of terrorism, and had been calling for cooperation to solve global tensions, and formulating a thesis on terrorism and religious extremism.

Speaking at the summit of the Organization for Security and Cooperation in Europe on 18 November 1999 in Istanbul, Nazarbayev had said: '... We must free ourselves decisively of the old stereotypes and lay the foundation for real global partnership. The implementation of such an approach guarantees success in resolving our own immediate problems, which seriously threaten today's global stability. I am referring to the proliferation of ethnic, national and religious conflicts. This dangerous phenomenon faces us, first and foremost, with unsettling socio-economic, humanitarian and ecological problems.'

Nazarbayev's speech at the millennium summit at the fifty-fifth session of the UN General Assembly in New York in 2000 turned out to be prophetic. He drew attention to the people's pleas and suffering due to procrastination over internal matters and Afghanistan, suggesting that this issue be raised beore the UN Security Council and speaking out for the need to develop an institution within the structure of the UN which, by analysis of the global situation, could forewarn of imminent conflicts, and come up with proposals for intervening in situations in the early stages and averting aggressive means of conflict resolution, effectively using preventative diplomacy.

Following the events of September 2001 in the USA, Nazarbayev said in an interview with a foreign journalist: 'In response to the events of September 11th and the subsequent antiterrorist operation in Afghanistan, our country was amongst the first to speak out in support of antiterrorist coalitions and has increased our readiness to afford all necessary means to the success of this operation: airfields, engineering, intelligence-gathering, humanitarian aid and other help. The war against terrorism began in Kazakhstan a long time before the tragedy of September 11th. From this very podium I warned the international community about the growing tension in Asia, about the situation in Afghanistan and about the approaching menace of international terrorism. Unfortunately, at the time no one listened. The events of the preceding years prove repeatedly that to eradicate terrorism it is necessary to eradicate the cause that is pushing people towards terrorism.' He called for state openness and transparency of mutually acceptable observance and monitoring of terrorist threats.

From the start of the antiterrorist operations in Afghanistan, Kazakhstan had abstained from participation and provided humanitarian aid. Kazakhstan expressed its readiness to send its specialists there (doctors, teachers, builders, engineers, etc) and – if invited by the UN – take part in international peacemaking missions in Afghanistan through the Kazakh peacemaking battalion 'Kazbat'.

The dramatic events of September 11th convinced Nazarbayev all the more of the necessity of initiating an inter-civilization dialogue. A most important step in this direction became the visit to Kazakhstan – a Muslim state par excellence – by the head of the Roman Catholic Church John Paul II, at the invitation of the President of Kazakhstan, literally ten days after the terrorist act in the city of New York. This visit, at its core, became the prologue for the First Congress of World and Traditional Religions which took place two years later, in September 2003, in Astana.

'The world is your home.'
Nursultan Nazarbayev and Pope
John Paul II, visiting Kazakhstan.

Among the major international forums organized in this period by Kazakhstan, the first Eurasian Economic Summit stands out. It took place under the auspices of the Davos Forum in Almaty in April 2000. Politicians and businessmen took part from more than forty states worldwide, also in the first Eurasian Media Forum, organized in April 2002 in the city of Almaty, which then became a yearly tradition.

But the real breakthrough for Kazakh diplomacy, which it had been striving towards for more than ten years, was the convening on 4 June 2002 of the first Conference on Interaction and Confidence Building Measures in Asia (CICA) in the city of Almaty. Sixteen countries partook in the CICA, as well as international organizations – the UN,

The First Congress of World and Traditional Religions, Astana, at the Bayterik monument.

the OSCE, the Arab League and observers from various countries. The Head of State called the summit of leaders from Asian states, 'the quintessential diplomatic doctrine of Kazakhstan'. The CICA Summit marked a new stage in international relations in Asia, demonstrating to the world the intellectual and organizational potential of Kazakhstan as an exemplar of a new architecture in foreign affairs at the start of the twenty-first century.

In September 2003, by Nazarbayev's initiative, Kazakhstan successfully hosted the First Congress of Leaders of World and Traditional Religions, gathering the spiritual hierarchs under a banner of open dialogue and rapprochement of civilizations.

The role of organizing and promoting Congress fell to Nazarbayev. Ahead of the launch, he shared his thoughts with a correspondent from the Japanese newspaper *Mainichi Shimbun*: 'I am not a supporter of

Samuel Huntington or Francis Fukuyama, featured in this magazine, or of the other popular research theories regarding the "conflict of civilizations" or other variations on the theme of "the end of history". Rather, my country – Kazakhstan – as in its past, now in its present, offers many examples of different civilizations and cultures living in close contact, each giving new impetus to the evolution of the other. The recent invitation of Pope John Paul II to Kazakhstan, where the majority of the population are Muslim, was eloquent proof of the achievement in our society of an atmosphere of common mutual respect and tolerance.

'Therefore, when identifying the sources of menace to mutual respect we must refrain from careless generalizations. We must not confuse "Muslim" and "terrorist" or identify the Taliban with the nation of Afghanistan. If one lets such matters drift, and fail to work towards mutual understanding, provoking a disorder of emotions and allowing mysterious figures to confuse peoples' religious sentiments, then even negligible disagreements and cultural stereotypes will lead to unpredictable catastrophe on a global scale. Therefore, it is the duty of all civilized people on this earth to do everything they can so religious, ethnic, racial wars, and confrontations of other kinds remain things of the past.'

Assessing the outcome of the Congress in an interview, Nazarbayev spoke of it being a historic breakthrough, and even the start of a new era of human development. He looked to it being held at regular intervals of no longer than three years.

The common thread running through these events, was Nazarbayev's plea for a collective effort to react to global crises and the threats confronting humanity in the twenty-first century.

He formed a relationship with leading international structures. The analysis and neutralization of threats of terrorism, organized crime, uncontrolled migration, and the trade in drugs and weapons of mass destruction became the remit of Kazakhstan cooperating with the UN, NATO and the OSCE.

The President laid stress on encouraging integration with neighbouring states. Kazakhstan's multilateral relationship was strengthened by the networks of the CIS, EurAsEC, CSTO, SCO, CAC and the ECO.

One result of the multisided international politics that flowed from these relationships was confirmed on 18 January 2005 in the historic agreement on the state border between Kazakhstan and Russia. With this signature, Kazakhstan ensured its terrestrial integrity in international law. The border is 7591 kilometres long, and is the most extensive of all Kazakhstan's frontiers with its neighbours and the longest terrestrial border in the world.

Nazarbayev spoke of it at the Third World Kurultai of Kazakhs, taking place on 29 September 2005. 'Our ancestors have always held matters relating to the land, to the living space for the nation, or to the defence of our external borders, as paramount. Here, in these first years of independence we have taken upon ourselves the resolution of this group of problems.

'As is well known, for a long period of its history Kazakhstan was stripped of its full potential to be an actually self-sufficient state. From the beginning, for two centuries, it was colonized by the tsars of Russia and then for more than seventy years was merely one of fifteen republics of the Soviet Union. With the collapse of the USSR, when each of these republics became a separate state, Kazakhstan was discovered to be not so small. The great spaces of Kazakhstan were looked upon with hungry eyes. Kazakhstan did not seek to label these spaces with proprietorial names. To those who know the motherland's history they were already known for what they were.

'In so many complex situations, when the fate of the nation was weighed on the scales of history, we used our discretion and reserve. Having opened discussions with all of our near and further neighbours, we confirmed our territorial integrity with them and strengthened external borders. First, we made the border with the People's Republic of China clear and signed a bilateral agreement with them. This was a real breakthrough since previously neither the Tsar of Russia nor the Soviet Union had been able to resolve the border debate in plain terms with China. In our case, the problem was resolved decisively once and for all, without any doubt or equivocation.

'The resolution of matters of borders and the signing of the agreement with two of our most important neighbours put an end to all the sporadic flare-ups over wild guesswork and claims aimed at subverting truth between our countries, which were historically amicable neighbours and partners.

'Many important agreements were also made in the south, with Uzbekistan, Kyrgyzstan and Turkmenistan. These consolidated the entire range of border conflict solutions.

'Thus, the Republic of Kazakhstan finally circumscribed the full length of its vast borders, 14,500 kilometres, leaving nothing in doubt, and strengthened its bilateral accords.

At the first CICA summit.

'If in this alone lies the most important of our achievements since gaining independence, we will be justified in the sight of our contemporaries and in the memory of future generations.'

In this potent context, the presidential elections took place in December 2005. In his appeal 'Kazakhstan – the Only Way is Forward!' with which Nazarbayev faced Kazakhs on the eve of the elections, the nation perceived a convincing example of the actualization of the 'Kazakh dream' as a national ideal: 'Having achieved success, we proved to the whole world that we are worthy of a great future ... But we cannot rest on this achievement. Whoever does not go forward remains without hope.

'We must go forward step by step, not swerving and not stepping back. Only thus is it possible to achieve our aims. I put this point to you. Together – calmly and confidently – we will go towards our future. I call upon you to go only forward! It is not possible to stop the future, but it is possible to plan for it. My plan is simple and achievable – care and kindness to our elders, work and prospects for the young, health and education for all, peace and harmony in each home. Kazakhstan will no longer be a country of crises, but a country where dreams are made. Kazakhstan – the only way is forward!'

The results of the elections, in which Nazarbayev prevailed with emphatic endorsement, reflected the nation's continuing support for the political approach of its leader.

Triumph. The Forum of Nazarbayev supporters, 5 December 2005.

11

A Formula for Competitiveness

The ceremony for the official swearing in of Nazarbayev as President, held on 11 January 2006, was especially significant for the Kazakh people.

It was Kazakhstan's first presidential inauguration of the twenty-first century. Furthermore, it was held in the capital's recently opened new state residency 'Akorda'. The residence, nestled in Astana's Left Bank with a total floor area of 36,720 square meters and a large dome some 80 meters in height, has come to symbolize independent Kazakhstan in the same way as the Kremlin does Russia or the White House America.

Another significant feature of the inauguration was the first performance of the anthem of Kazakhstan, based on the well-known and much-loved popular song 'My Kazakhstan' ('Menıñ Qazaqstanım'), written by the composer Shamshi Kaldayakov with lyrics by Jumeken Najimedenov.

Astana, Akorda, 11 January 2006.

Түпнұсқа

Жаңа нұсқасы

МЕНІҢ ҚАЗАҚСТАНЫМ

МЕНІҢ ҚАЗАҚСТАНЫМ

Әні – Шәмші Қалдаяқовтікі,
Сөзі - Жұмекен Нәжімеденовтікі

Әні – Шәмші Қалдаяқовтікі,
Сөзі - Жұмекен Нәжімеденовтікі

Алтын күн аспаны,
Алтын дән даласы.
Думанды бастады,
Далама қарашы.
Кең екен жер деген,
Жерге дән шықты ғой.
Дән егіп терлеген,
Қазағым мықты ғой.

Алтын күн аспаны,
Алтын дән даласы.
Ерліктің дастаны –
Еліме қарашы!
Ежелден ер деген,
Даңқымыз шықты ғой.
Намысын бермеген,
Қазағым мықты ғой!

Қайырмасы:

Қайырмасы:

Менің елім, менің елім,
Гүлің болып егілемін,
Жырың болып төгілемін, елім,
Туған жерім менің – Қазақстаным.

Менің елім, менің елім,
Гүлің болып егілемін,
Жырың болып төгілемін, елім,
Туған жерім менің – Қазақстаным!

Сағымды далам бар,
Сабырлы көлім бар.
Қарандар, жарандар,
Осындай елім бар.
Қарсы алған уақытты,
Ежелгі досындай.
Біздің ел бақытты,
Біздің ел осындай.

Ұрпаққа жол ашқан,
Кең байтақ жерім бар.
Бірлігі жарасқан,
Тәуелсіз елім бар.
Қарсы алған уақытты,
Мәңгілік досындай.
Біздің ел бақытты,
Біздің ел осындай!

'It shall be so!' The final version of the lyrics of Kazakhstan's national anthem.

Just days beforehand, the President had appealed to his MPs to consider a change of national anthem. The Head of State's letter of proposal was considered at a joint session of the two parliamentary chambers on 6 January 2006. 'It has long been clear that the national anthem adopted in the wake of Kazakhstan's independence has not found its way into the hearts of the people. However, in my travels all over the country, I have repeatedly witnessed how Kazakhstanis of all ages have been inspired by the song "My Kazakhstan". For many a generation this song has been an unofficial anthem, and I believe that it is time to give it official status … I propose to Parliament that it considers a version of this song as a possible anthem for the Republic of Kazakhstan, one that preserves the original's melody with a few changes to its text. Without claiming any authorship, I present to you my

The door to the country
by sea. Port Aktau.

updated version.' 'My Kazakhstan' was a fitting choice of national anthem, as it was the song closest to the heart of the country's people. A number of articles had appeared in the press which showed citizens to be in favour of a change of anthem. In 2001, the issue was even raised in Parliament.

The President, whose custom it was never to delegate matters of importance to others, was constantly involved in the new anthem's development, himself making modernizing additions and changes to the original lyrics, concering the idea of independence and the indestructible unity of the Kazakh people.

Nazarbayev, well versed in his country's language and culture, is the author of many original and accomplished works of poetry, including the lyrics of the much-loved popular songs 'Elym Menyn', 'Zherym Menym', 'Ushkonyr', and 'Saryarka'. In 2010, on his family's initiative, *The Light of the Soul*, a limited-edition collection of his poetry, was released, including more than seventy poems written over many years.

However, he would never consider himself a poet, and his lyrical explorations are modest, purely for personal creative expression.

The inauguration ceremony was attended by a record number of guests from the official delegations of more than seventy countries, as well as international and intergovernmental organizations, such as the UN, OSCE, CIS, CSTO, SCO, EurAsEC, and ECO.

The content of the President's inaugural address was grand in scale and intent: 'It is my aim, and has been for a long time, to make Kazakhstan one of the fifty most competitive countries in the world within the next decade. Development is defined not just by the economy, by per capita income or GDP. I am talking about a state developed in four different ways – economically, politically, socially and culturally. This requires an integrated programme involving serious economic, administrative, political and legal change. A lot of work is ahead of us, and I will endeavour to use the time given me by the people to achieve these ends. I must do justice to this carte blanche with a strong political will and a clear articulation of my priorities.'

The President's main idea was that in the twenty-first century, success would come to the countries that could reform fastest and most extensively, and that any attempt to preserve an island of prosperity reliant solely on natural resources was futile. 'The global economy of today is a relentless struggle in which one does not ever win a lasting victory. It must be constantly defended,' Nazarbayev stressed. 'A nation's competitiveness depends on its ability to develop and evolve.'

The final details of his strategy were to be found in his address 'A New Kazakhstan in a New World' on 28 February 2007, in which President Nazarbayev formulated thirty state political directives, grouped under six main priorities: integration into the world economy through the identification and use of existing competitive advantages and the creation of new ones; management of economic growth and sustainability through diversification, the development of infrastructure and the creation of centres for high-tech industry; ensuring international standards of education and professional training for the development of the workforce; a modern social politics oriented to the demands and needs of the people and the creation of jobs; political and administrative development based on the logic of this new phase; and a new regional and geopolitical responsibility for Kazakhstan.

Following this, Nazarbayev continued to make large-scale reforms to complement his strategic objectives for competitive development.

Kazakhstan's railways –
the foundation of modern
infrastructure.

In 2006, a State Commission was established on the President's orders for the development of democratic reforms in Kazakhstan, the lawful successor of the Body for the Development of Proposals for the Further Democratization and Development of Civil Society (2002–4) and the National Commission on Democracy and Civil Society (2004–5). The principal difference between this State Commission and former platforms for national dialogue was that this was led by the President. Opening the Commission on 24 March 2006, he said: 'In my address to the nation, I outlined the main priorities of our development strategy, the implementation of which will enable Kazakhstan to take its rightful place among the most competitive countries in the world. I believe, and I think you agree with me, that such large-scale challenges can only be achieved by effective government bodies, the development of political institutions, constructive political parties, NGOs and other civil organizations which guarantee the rights and freedoms of citizens. As such, we are determined to continue the democratic transformation and political modernization of this country ... I will be leading the Commission in this regard.'

In the State Commission there were representatives of Parliament, the government, political parties, public figures and leading experts of the country. The President had the task of identifying the best ways to implement reforms that would further democratize the political system, including the creation of the legal framework for decentralization and local self-government, transparency and efficiency in the judicial system, increased public support for NGOs and political parties occupying Parliament, and so on. The result of this work was the document entitled 'Guidelines for Political Reform in the Republic of Kazakhstan for 2007–2008'.

On 16 May, Nazarbayev addressed a joint session of his Parliament and introduced a bill on amendments to the Constitution, developed by the State Commission. 'Today is a historic day for Kazakhstan's democracy. Here is, for your consideration, a draft law on amendments and additions to the Constitution. This document is the conclusion of an enormous amount of work on the implementation of a national programme of political reforms, and profound changes in the legal environment of the country ... I suggest we adopt these changes to the Constitution, retaining a presidential republic but significantly enhancing the powers of Parliament. This model transforms our country from a presidential system to one that is parliamentary-presidential.'

The law 'On Amendments to the Constitution of the Republic of Kazakhstan', adopted on 21 May 2007, ensured the further devolution of power from the President to Parliament. First of all, Parliament was granted the right to participate directly in the formation of the government, meaning the Prime Minister would now only be appointed with the consent of the majority of the Majilis. Parliament also gained the right to form two-thirds of the Constitutional Council, the Accounts Committee which controlled the spending of the budget, and the Central Election Commission. Now, to carry through a vote of no confidence in the government, the Majilis only needed more than half the votes rather than the previous majority of two-thirds. Also, in the long term, calculating the state budget and control over its execution would also be a prerogative of Parliament.

In turn, the Presidential institution also underwent a number of changes. The President received the right to initiate legislation, to appoint fifteen senators instead of seven, and also to nominate seven members of the Assembly of Peoples of Kazakhstan for the Majilis. In 2005 the Assembly, celebrating its tenth anniversary, was renamed the Assembly of People of Kazakhstan, gaining constitutional status and the right to delegate their representatives to the lower house of Parliament.

At the same time local representative bodies were given more power: in accordance with the presidential decree of 4 June 2007 'On the Appointment of *Akims* in Regions, Cities of Regional Importance and City Districts' the *akims* were appointed with the approval of *maslikhats*. A similar scheme was also proposed by the President regarding the *akims*

One united family.

of certain regions; now the President approved their appointment with the corresponding *maslikhats*. Moreover, *maslikhats* attained a greater influence on the *akims*, because they too could now express confidence as a simple majority rather than needing two-thirds of the vote.

In general, the constitutional reform and subsequent elections to the Majilis of 18 August 2007 marked a new stage in the political development of Kazakhstan, following other important political events that took place during this period. On 4 July 2006 the country's the two main political parties united; Otan and Asar had made up the core of the People's Coalition for Nazarbayev during his presidential campaign. The ongoing process of consolidating the forces of the pro-presidential bloc continued in November and December 2006, when the Otan joined the Civil and Agrarian Party of Kazakhstan. In December, an updated and bigger party was renamed as the People's Democratic Party, Nur Otan. It was chaired by President Nazarbayev.

12

Leader

With the first decade of the twenty-first century behind it, Kazakhstan once again faced difficulty. The scale of the impending global economic crisis had not been seen since the time of the Great Depression of the 1930s or the financial meltdown after World War II. At the end of 2007, the avalanche-like recession destroyed a whole range of leading financial institutions, stopping huge industrial companies in their tracks, bankrupting several governments, exacerbating energy and food crises in various regions, and dooming tens of millions of people to unemployment. In view of Kazakhstan's close-knit integration into international economic networks, the effects of the pandemic crisis were inevitable. The young republic faced a real threat of financial collapse, which would massively affect quality of life and could lead to mass impoverishment.

Affection demonstrated and exchanged.

Fortunately, the crisis was expected and did not catch Kazakhstan unawares. In March 2007, in his message to the nation, 'New Kazakhstan in the New World', Nazarbayev warned local financiers, remembering the pitfalls of dependence on external credit: 'Our banks rely heavily on external finances and this can lead to an uncontrollable increase in the country's total external debts.' Justification for this concern soon came, when, playing with surplus profits rather than reselling external bonds to internal creditors, certain players in the financial market turned out to be very irresponsible.

The world crisis became openly alarming in the middle of 2008. In many countries the size of industry shrunk, with businesses partially or fully grinding to a halt. This led to a sharp fall in demand for raw materials.

Each day the world's media bore ominous news. In the USA seventeen major banks were bankrupt, including leading investment banks Bear Stearns, Lehman Brothers Holdings Inc. and Merrill Lynch, leading to unprecedented mortgage collapse; the debts of European banks placed many European Union countries on the brink of bankruptcy and created a real threat to the world bank system; in China, the number of unemployed grew to 20 million people; the recession in Japan grew three times worse than in the USA; and in Turkey unemployment gripped 13.5 per cent of the population, a level which had not been seen for half a century. Major world brands previously considered unshakeable, such as Volkswagen AG, General Motors and Nokia, suffered due to declining demand for their product and were forced to cut tens of thousands of jobs.

Although it conducted an open economic political strategy and was the most integrated amongst the CIS countries in the world economy, at the time Kazakhstan was still addressing its dependence on raw materials. These events therefore did not pass without effect.

As the first signs of the crisis appeared, Nazarbayev focused the government's attention on implementing actions aimed at minimizing the negative consequences. As he had warned, the most vulnerable sectors were the manufacturing industry, commercial banks, the property market and, linked with these, mortgage and loan institutions.

The focus of Nazarbayev's state-of-the-nation address, 'Growth of the Prosperity of the Kazakh Citizen – the Chief Aim of State Policy', given at the joint congress in Parliament on 6 February 2008, was on countering the crisis. In response to the most pressing challenges, Nazarbayev identified the main priorities: to guarantee the stability of

The wellbeing of the citizen –
the chief mission of the state.

the financial sector; to strengthen the state's influential and responsible participation in international oil and energy markets; to develop infrastructure of the economy and – first and foremost – electro-energy and transport infrastructure, which were being 'left behind in the development of the economy of Kazakhstan'; to strengthen the agricultural industrial sector on the basis of expanding export-orientated agricultural departments; and finally to fully support businesses. In the face of this, he outlined the state's long-term policy of social protection: raising the pensions and pay of state employees.

Nazarbayev's rational perspective on the worsening situation became a necessity in the interests of public stability. He compiled a thesis on the re-evaluation of the reasons behind the world crisis: 'to concentrate on extremes and to point fingers is unproductive; now it is more important to focus on identifying far-reaching defects in the system, which have already caused so many huge world cataclysms and, most importantly, to find ways to eliminate them totally. The crisis arrived on our doorstep from outside. It is not sourced from within this country but from the imbalance in the world economy ... it is not possible to flee the crisis or see everything before it happens ... We will overcome it and, from this, we will become an ever stronger and more prosperous state.'

Above:
In conference, on the steppes and at play.

Left:
On horseback, for a contest of ferocious kokpar.

On 13 October 2008, a parliamentary congress was held where regional akims, as well as those of the cities of Astana and Almaty, and heads of national companies attended. There, the President told Parliament to develop a complex anti-crisis programme. On the Head of State's direction, Parliament called for the stabilization of the financial sector, the resolution of problems in the property market, the support of small- and medium-sized businesses, the stimulation of agriculture and the implementation of industrial and infrastructure projects.

On 25 November, the government initiated its anti-crisis programme. The huge fund set aside for the project exceeded 2.2 trillion tenge, more than half of which (1.2 trillion tenge, or 10 billion dollars) were set aside from the National Fund; compared with similar anti-crisis

packages, it was the largest in the CIS. The fund was split into five principal directions: towards the stabilization of the financial sector, the defence of the interests of investors and the harmonization of the property market, the support of small- and medium-sized business, the development of agriculture, the diversification of the economy and the realization of infrastructure projects. In addition, the government set aside 11,000 educational grants and 40,000 reduced-rate loans with the aim of protecting the country's youth.

On Nazarbayev's direction the National Welfare Fund Samruk-Kazyna was founded through the confluence of two major state holding companies: Samruk and Kazyna. Their aim was to implement anti-crisis programmes and use the funds set aside for this effectively. In addition, the temporary acquisition of shares of the four leading commercial banks – the National Bank, Alliance Bank, BTA bank and Kazkommertsbank – occurred, successfully stabilizing Kazakhstan's banking system. In February 2009 the National Bank achieved an important defensive measure by devaluing the tenge, thus strengthening the position of local commodity producers: their products became cheaper and, as such, more competitive in foreign markets. Furthermore, since 2009 a new tax code was put into action, lessening the burden on the non-energy sector.

At the same time, measures were taken for the social defence of the population. In many countries a wave of mass unemployment rolled out, but Kazakhstan increased the level of pay of its public sector workers and pensions by 25 per cent. Though the ethics behind reviewing previously made decisions were questioned, Nazarbayev did not break his promises: in his 2009 state-of-the-nation address, he declared that in 2010, public sector pay, stipends and pensions would increase by more than 25 per cent and in 2011, by more than 30 per cent. These promises were carried out.

The signing of a memorandum between government and local councils became a crucial measure for social welfare; its aim was not to allow those in power to cut jobs. The President placed responsibility on all executive departments of government: 'An ability to provide a sufficient level of employment should be the basic indicator of whether members of the government and *akims* are capable of guaranteeing the ongoing growth of Kazakhstan's economy.' A programme entitled 'Roadmap' was unveiled for the construction of roads, erecting sites of social importance and developing infrastructure of communal-living households; this allowed the creation of approximately 400,000 new employment positions and provided almost 100,000 people with the opportunity to gain a secondary qualification for free. Thanks to large-scale state support – providing building companies with credit and refinancing mortgage institutions – the property market was stabilized

In the country's Parliament. The timely message to the nation of Kazakhstan, 6 February 2008.

and tens of thousands of new healthcare and educational institutions were saved. Nearly 340 billion tenge was put towards supporting small- and medium-sized business. As a result, the level of unemployment fell to 6.5 per cent.

Kazakhstan not only stood firm before the economic storm, but, without slowing, continued to realize its long term goals (the Kazakhstan-2030 Strategy, the Strategy of Industrial-Innovation Development due for completion in 2015, and so on). There were several significant events in achieving these strategic aims, conducted in partnership with international financial institutions and foreign investors: the Turkmenistan-Uzbekistan-Kazakhstan-China gas pipeline; the Kenkiyak-Kumkol oil pipe line; the gas manufacturing factory at the Kumkol oil field; the huge North-South voltage transmission line, 1100 kilometres in length; the locomotive plant in the city of Astana; Astana-Burabay – the first world-class motorway in Kazakhstan, and others.

On the tenth anniversary of the new capital of Kazakhstan, Astana's achievements were plain for all to see; celebration on a national and international level bore witness to this.

Drawing upon the positive implementation of the anti-crisis programme, Nazarbayev formulated a new challenge: to divise a strategy

for Kazakhstan's inclusion in the fifty most financially competitive states in the world.

Meeting with the Prime Minister and the Head of the Presidential Administration.

On 6 March 2009 his message to the nation, 'Past the Crisis and onto Renewal and Development', stated that solutions would not be limited to problems created by the world crisis; they would, more importantly, focus on the formation of infrastructure for the post-crisis development of the country and increased competitiveness in the national economy.

The evening before he gave this message, Nazarbayev made another set of notes: 'There are two points: either we sit and passively watch as the crisis destroys everything, or we actively work though the crisis to the future. If we do not escape the harmful effects of the crisis, we will lose the luxuries we have had until now. We will destroy the platform on which the new can be built ...[thus] we propose the idea of a plan for radical regeneration, so that we can realize our full potential. We will act, and we will win.'

The President identified what was needed for the post-crisis restructuring of the economy: the formation of competitive human capital, the improvement of the business climate and boosting entrepreneurial activity in the country, the guarantee of administrative and judicial reforms and the long-term democratization of Kazakh society.

The above priorities formed the foundation of the Strategic Plan for the Development of the Republic of Kazakhstan until 2020, heralding the subsequent implementation of the Kazakhstan-2030 Strategy. At its core was the State Programme of Accelerated Industrial-Innovation

Development for the years 2010–14, which integrated the essential approaches of the Strategy for Industrial-Innovation Development due for completion in 2015, the programmes of cluster initiatives, the Thirty Corporate Leaders of Kazakhstan programme, and others.

Understanding that the sources of the crisis lay far outside the boundaries of Kazakhstan, Nazarbayev involved himself in international discussions on the reasons behind and means for speedily overcoming the crisis.

In January 2009, the President gave a speech at the beginning of his visit to India at the Kazakhstan-Indian Business Forum. He addressed the expediency of introducing a new world currency and of changing the principles by which the world financial system was controlled: 'The future world directly depends on the existence of a fair and universal international currency ... it must be managed by the UN and controlled by a specially created commission.'

At the end of January, Nazarbayev unveiled his approach to the issue at the World Economic Forum in Davos, Switzerland, in a series of meetings with other heads of state and leading international experts. His ideas were presented in their final form in his article 'Keys to the Crisis', published in the *Russian Newspaper* on 2 February 2009.

Although the possibility of a supranational world currency had been previously considered, the urgency of the Kazakh leader's suggestion, articulated during an international crisis, attracted interest. The initiative shown by Kazakhstan resonated in the international arena and became a subject of discussion amongst leading world experts.

Amongst the first to respond were Russian academics. A letter from the Academics of the Russian Academy of Sciences, O.T. Bogomolov, N. Petrakov and S. Glazyev said: 'The suggestions made in the article on reforming international monetary and financial relations will undoubtedly become a subject of serious discussion, not only in our country but in international scientific, financial and business circles. The posing of these questions is crucial to forming a new architecture for a global monetary and financial system. Your suggestions for their resolution, mutually beneficial in essence, are the only plausible means of finding a way out of the global economic crisis.'

Later, from the podium of the second Astana Economic Forum on the 'Economic Security of Eurasia in a Climate of International Risk', taking place in the Kazakh capital in March 2009, the Head of State justified his approaches in his quest for a post-Soviet outlook. In terms of the prospects of the EurAsEC, the President stated that its members should create an integrated financial system whereby a unique supranational cash-free account-based unit of currency could be introduced, the strength of which would not depend on fluctuations in international currencies.

Nazarbayev developed his ideas in a range of articles and interviews published throughout 2009: 'In the Long Term There is No Real Alternative' (*Izvestia*, 19 March), 'Five Ways' (*Izvestia*, 22 September) and others. Important additions to world economic theory also came with his books, *The Strategy of Becoming a Post-Industrial Society and a Partnership of Civilizations* and *The Global Energy Strategy for Sustainable Development in the Twenty-first Century*, published between 2008 and 2011. Though the Kazakh leader's aims cannot be realized immediately, we hope that one day the world will take on Nazarbayev's suggestions and set up a supranational currency.

The Conference on Interaction and Confidence-building Measures in Asia, the idea for which Nazarbayev first announced at the forty-seventh session of the UN General assembly in 1992, turned into a genuine mechanism for collective security on a continental scale. By the start of 2011, CICA had united twenty states, covering 90 per cent of the territory of Asia, encompassing half of the earth's population. Time has proven CICA's significance, with the political dialogue between Asian states constantly gaining momentum. Not stopping at this,

Above:
Nazarbayev uses the popular press for his analysis 'Keys to the Crisis'.

Left:
'With the past in mind, stride into the future.' A montage of the books of Nazarbayev.

Adorning the open spaces of the capital, Akorda, the Presidential Palace in Astana, soars into the empyrean.

Kazakhstan intends to spread CICA's ideas across the whole of Asia. In the long term, the CICA, using Nazarbayev's ideas, should form the basis for the organization of security in Asia.

The Congress of Leaders of World and Traditional Religions, which met on Kazakh land for the third time in 2009, has become a natural and efficient part of contemporary global interfaith dialogue. It plays a significant role in facilitating the growth of mutual understanding among spiritual leaders, religions and nations.

The President's years of activity in terms of initiatives for international integration bore fruit; they were crowned with the creation of the Customs Union of Kazakhstan, Russia and Belarus in 2009 and the Eurasian Economic Community in 2011. For Kazakhstan, integration meant the potential for its businesses to reach a market of more than 150 million people; a significant growth in GDP; an increase of industrial work and in the quality of imports; an improvement of the economic system and the implementation of modern, progressive standards of living for the entire population; and, chiefly, the creation

of a single economic space with freedom of movement for trade, services, workforce and capital.

Having signed this invaluable pact, Kazakhstan accepted the 2010 mandate and led the major European organization, the OSCE. Kazakhstan became the first country of the CIS, the first Turkic country, the first historically Islamic country, and most importantly, the first Asian country to lead the OSCE.

This display of international trust had a deep symbolic meaning for Kazakhstan, essentially confirming its self-perception as an undoubted leader on the international stage, a position our nation had gone towards step by step since the first days of independence.

At the celebratory ceremony on 15 December 2009 on the Day of Independence, the President, underlining the significance of this mandate, said, 'Kazakhstan's governance of the OSCE has become the crown of all our achievements since our independence. This is one of the highest forms of recognition of our collective work. Over the centuries, the Kazakh nation has never attracted this degree of international

'Towards a new architecture for the global financial system' was the President's theme at the sixty-second UN General Assembly in 2007.

attention. With this event, Kazakhstan has emerged as a self-sufficient state. This is our greatest achievement.'

In the Vienna meeting of the Permanent Council of the OSCE, at Kazakhstan's inauguration as Head of the OSCE, Nazarbayev included Kazakhstan's detailed mission statement in a video message to its participants: 'The motto of Kazakh leadership will be the four Ts: Trust, Tradition, Transparency and Tolerance. The first is mutual trust. The second is the commitment to the founding principles and aims of the OSCE. The third is for absolute openness in international relations, free from double standards, with the aim of constructive cooperation to overcome threats to our security. The fourth is to strengthen intercultural and dialogue, which has special significance in the modern world.'

Due to problems in the organization's management, the participants of the OSCE had not convened for more than ten years since the 1999 summit in Istanbul. However, immediately after its inauguration, Kazakhstan organized an urgent OSCE summit.

Even before then, Nazarbayev had spoken out several times of his concern for the prospects of the Organization for Security and

At the podium of the second Astana Economic Forum.

A formal lecture at Nazarbayev University.

Cooperation in Europe. And so, at the OSCE Meeting of Intercultural, Interreligious and Interethnic Understanding held in June 2006 in Almaty, he noted that Kazakhstan felt a high degree of responsibility for the future of the organization, which was currently not prospering. He called for a review of the organizational structure and management of the OSCE, particularly taking the interests of new states into account.

Nazarbayev also called for the reformation of the UN amidst new global issues. At the sixty-second session of the UN General Assembly held in New York in September 2007 he said: 'We support cooperative efforts for the reformation of the UN. Kazakhstan is a firm ally of those states that are prepared to expand the role of the UN, as it is the only international organ capable of having an effect on matters of war and peace. In our opinion, the expansion of the Security Council should encompass all nations, with fair geographical representation and respect for the sovereignty of each individual state. The reform should also help the Security Council's efforts to increase its transparency and accountability. The General Assembly should have a central role as the chief advisory, administrative and governing organ of the UN.'

As was expected, the overwhelming majority of the countries of the OSCE were in full support of Nazarbayev's initiative. On 3 August, the OSCE's Council of Ministers of Foreign Affairs eventually took the decision to hold the summit in Astana: it would be in December 2010. On 5 August, Nazarbayev underlined the symbolical nature of the event, as thirty-five years ago, on 1 August 1975, the Helsinki Final Act had been signed. The leader of Kazakhstan was confident that the meeting would allow the organization to adapt to modern realities in full and to demonstrate to the world community the successful development of the OSCE 'from Helsinki to Astana'.

The OSCE summit in Astana.
December 2010.

The Astana summit of the OSCE, beginning on 1 December 2010, brought together nearly 2,500 delegates from fifty-two states and twelve partner organizations, including the UN, NATO, the CIS and others.

More than 1500 representatives of the world's media arrived to cover the event. The informal but businesslike tone used by Nazarbayev at the summit encouraged participants to leave fruitless quibbles at the door and engage in constructive discussion.

The hot debate that unfolded at the summit was not unexpected. But, as an experienced pilot who knew how to navigate between diametrically opposed positions, Nazarbayev managed to achieve a general consensus, which was reflected in the Astana declaration. As he went on to say, 'this is our shared, true, historic success, which answers our nations' hopes for a safer and better world. I believe that the Astana declaration will kick-start the formation of a community of Euro-Atlantic and Eurasian security. Following the results of the summit and Kazakhstan's governance of the OSCE on the whole, it is hoped that many more of such summits will be held here.'

Kazakhstan's chairmanship of the Organization for Security and Cooperation in Europe was a major diplomatic victory, and reflected

Kazakhstan's increased international authority, one of its many successes in the years of independence.

The most important result of Kazakhstan's leadership of the OSCE was that it gave new life to the organization's development. The OSCE, being the only security structure encompassing all the countries of Europe and North America, could finally fulfil its role as a leading dialogue platform between states of the East and West. 'The Spirit of Astana' entered the international political lexicon, becoming a symbol of shared efforts to construct a better world, founded on the principles of trust, agreement, tolerance and unity in all their forms.

Nazarbayev gained international recognition for his exclusive role in constructing a modern, strong and flourishing state, and was presented with the status of Leader of the Nation. Despite his modest protestations, on 14 June 2010 the deputies of Parliament unanimously voted in support of the referendum. The resolution was a logical one since long before this, many countries, in respect for the personality, work and service of Nazarbayev, had proposed similar commemorative signs.

Kazakhstan celebrated twenty years of independence in 2011. The occasion was marked for its people and their leader by a range of important events. On the eve of the coming 2011 – on 23 December 2010 – in the city of Ust-Kamenogorsk, a national forum took place; here, the expediency of holding a referendum on whether the powers of the Head of State should be extended until 2020 was raised. The idea received broad support amongst Kazakhs. In a month, more than 5 million citizens had signed the referendum – more than half the voters in the country. Parliament's support for the initiative was also clear, formalized in changes and additions to the Constitution.

The notion of a referendum was unexpected for the President. At a meeting with deputies of Parliament, leaders of political parties and representatives of the intelligentsia on 20 January in Akorda, he said: 'You have put me in a difficult position and I am speechless.'

In the end Nazarbayev declined the parliamentary initiative. When Parliament intended to keep the new law anyway, the Head of State was forced to call on the Constitutional Council, which recognized that the law was inconsistent with the Constitution.

At the Constitutional Council Nazarbayev appealed to the nation, expressing his deep sense of conscience to all Kazakhs. He spoke in support of the referendum, but explained that, as President and guarantor of the Constitution, he could not and did not want to create

Kazakhstan's celebration of twenty years of independence in 2011 was marked – among other events – by a national forum in the city of Ust- Kamenogorsk.

a precedent which could be abused by future generations of politicians: 'I suggest that all of us look at this situation, not as "accepting or refusing", but as a historical lesson in democracy, which teaches us about our own lives, as a lesson which ensures the President and the nation can still trust in the Constitution.'

On 28 January 2011, the President gave his next message to the nation, entitled 'We will Build the Future Together'. On 11 February, at the Thirteenth Congress of the National-Democratic Party Nur Otan, delegates unanimously proposed Nazarbayev as their candidate for leadership of the party and for the post of President of the Republic of Kazakhstan, to which the he agreed.

On 3 April 2011, elections for the President of the Republic of Kazakhstan took place. On 5 April 2011, the Central Election Commission announced the final results – Nazarbayev received 95.55 per cent of the votes of all those taking part in the election.

At the end of that year, the deputies of the lower chamber of Parliament took the decision to voluntarily dissolve itself and hold the elections in the Majilis. After consulting with speakers at the lower chambers of Parliament and receiving the Prime Minister's support for the decision, the President declared, 'the renewal of Parliament is necessary for the large-scale modernization happening in this country.

If another crisis comes, it would once again complicate the work of the leadership, the government and the regions of this country, and so we must never sit still.' Soon after this, a high law-making body was created and elections in the Majilis and *maslikhat* were set for 15 January 2010. Representatives of three political parties took part – the national democratic party Nur Otan, the Democratic Party of Kazakhstan Ak Zhol, and the Communist National Party of Kazakhstan.

At the event celebrating twenty years of Kazakh independence, Nazarbayev spoke with pride of Kazakhstan's sovereign development during that period. He directed the glance of the nation to the future, underlining that, in the context of unstoppable change across the globe, there stood before the country the task of finding new approaches to positioning itself in global civilization; the need to conduct self-critical evaluation of its own potential, factoring in all pluses and minuses; and the need to develop Kazakhstan's prospects from the point of view of developing in the modern globalizing world.

In the first years of its independence, Kazakhstan, having endured many difficulties, had stood firm and now the country looked confidently towards the future. The nation's many achievements prove that there are no irresolvable challenges or unachievable aims. A clear understanding of potential and the desire to win always prevails.

These victories would not have been possible without the strategic route taken by the Kazakhs, consolidated by the First President of the country Nursultan Nazarbayev: 'International support and the trust of our nation, constantly shown to me throughout all these years, have been my highest reward. It inspired and inspires me in the most difficult times, of which there have been many. Forever more, while health and strength suffice, I will labour for the good of the motherland and the nation of Kazakhstan!'

It is often difficult to evaluate the full scope and significance of events in the present. This is the prerogative of future generations. The nature of human memory is such that it retains only the brightest and most significant moments, often reducing full historical epochs to one short name. And, who knows, maybe the period of the birth and establishment of Kazakhstan will someday be remembered thus: 'Nursultanyn Nuryl Zholi' (the radiant path of Nursultan).

Appointments, Honours and Awards

Appointments

The First President of the Republic of Kazakhstan – Elbasi (leader of the nation)

The Supreme Commander of the Armed Forces of the Republic Kazakhstan

The President of the Security Union of the Republic of Kazakhstan

The President of the International Association of Kazakhs

The President of the Assembly of Kazakh Nations

The President of the Nur Otan National Democratic Party

The President of the Union of Foreign Investors under the President of the Republic of Kazakhstan

The President of the Union of Entrepreneurship under the President of the Republic of Kazakhstan

The President of the High Advisory Council of Nazarbayev University

Qualifications and Titles

Economics Ph.D dissertation: *Potential Economy of Raw Materials (on the Materials of Kazakhstan)*. Specialty 08.00.05 – Economics, Planning and Organization of the Management of the National Economy and its Departments. Academy of Public Sciences under the Central Committee of the CPSU, Moscow, USSR. Completed 15 July 1990

Economics Ph.D dissertation: *Strategic Resource Management under the Conditions of the Implementation and Development of Market Relations*. Specialty 08.00.05 – Economics, Planning and Organization of the Management of the National Economy and its Departments. Russian

Academy of Management, Moscow, USSR. Completed 29 December 1992

Honorary doctor of the Kazakh State University named after al-Farabi (Kazakhstan). November 1992

Honorary professor of the International Kazakh-Turkish University named after Khoja Ahmed Yasawi (Kazakhstan). April 1993

Academic of the International Academy of Engineers, Russia. April 1993

Academic of the Academy of Social Sciences (Russia). April 1993

Acknowledgement from Columbia University of outstanding service (USA). February 1994

Honorary professor of the Kazakh State University named after al-Farabi (Kazakhstan). March 1994

Honorary doctor of the Kazakh Institute of Management, Economics and Forecasting (Kazakhstan). October 1996

Honorary academic of the Nuri Khujand National Academy (Tajikistan). February 1997

Academic of the International Academy of Information (Russia). May 1997

Honorary member of the National Academy of Applied Sciences (Russia). December 1997

Academic of the International Academy of Information Technology (Belarus). June 1998

Honorary doctor of Political Sciences from Bilkent University (Turkey). June 1998

Honorary doctor of Economics from the Academy of Economic Sciences of Romania (Romania). September 1998

Honorary doctor of the Kazakh National Medical University named after S.D Asfendiyarov (Kazakhstan). March 1998

Honorary academic of the International Academy of Arts (Russia). January 1999

Member of the International Academy of Information (Russia). March 1999

Honorary Professor of the Institute of Economics and Management (Russia). April 1999

Honorary member of the Academy of Cosmonauts named after K.E. Tsiolkovsky (Russia). April 1999

Academic of the International Academy of Technological Sciences (Russia). October 1999

Foreign member of the International Academy of Technological Sciences (Switzerland). October 1999

Honorary professor of the Kazakh National Agrarian University (Kazakhstan). November 1999

Honorary doctor of the Mongolian State University (Mongolia). November 1999

Honorary member of the International Academy of Arts (Russia). April 2000

Honorary doctor of the Belarus State University (Belarus). May 2000

Honorary doctor of the Eurasian State University named after L.N. Gumilev (Kazakhstan). June 2000

Honorary doctor of the Russian Academy of Civil Service under the President of the Russian Federation (Russia). May 2000

Honorary professor of the Yerevan State University (Armenia). May 2001

Honorary doctor of the Kyrgyzstan National State University (Kyrgyzstan). July 2001

Honorary member of the Academy of Sciences of the Islamic World (Jordan). April 2002

Honorary doctor of Peking University (China). December 2002

Honorary doctor of Moscow State University named after M.V. Lomonosov (Russia). February 2003

Honorary degree in the field of Applied Technology (Canada). June 2003

Honorary professor of the University of Cambridge (Great Britain). April 2004

Honorary professor of the Moscow Institute of Steel and Alloy (Russia). April 2005

Honorary doctor of the Tajik National State University (Tajikistan). September 2007

Honorary doctor of the Christian University named after D.A. Cantemir (Romania). November 2007

Honorary doctor of the Moscow Institute for International Relations (Russia). 20 December 2007

Honorary president of the Eurasian Economics Students Club (Kazakhstan). April 2008

Honorary doctor of the University of Okan, Turkey. October 2009

Honorary professor of the Kazakh National University of Arts (Kazakhstan). May 2010

Honorary doctor of the Kiev National University named after T.G. Shevchenko (Ukraine). September 2010

Honorary doctor of the Korean University (Republic of Korea). April 2010

Honorary doctor of the Vietnam State University (Vietnam). November 2011

State Honours of the USSR

Orders

1972 – Order of the Badge of Honour

1980 – Order of the Red Banner of Labour

Medals

1970 – Jubilee Medal for Valiant Labour in Commemoration of the Hundredth Anniversary of Lenin's Birth

1984 – Medal For Development of Virgin Lands

1988 – Jubilee Medal for Seventy Years of the Armed Forces of the USSR

Other Honours

1961 – Title of 'Drummer Communist Labour'

1962 – Honorary diploma of the Komsomol

1967 – 'Sign of the Komsomol'

1968 – Title of 'Outstanding Student in the USSR Socialist Metallurgical Competition'

1971 – Honorary diploma of the Supreme Council of Kazakhstan

State Honours of the Republic of Kazakhstan

Orders

1996 – Order of the Golden Eagle Special Sample

2012 – Title of Halyk Kaharmany (National Hero)

Medals

1998 – Astana Jubilee Medal

2001 – Kazakhstan Respublikasynyn Tauelsizdigine 10 Zhyl Jubilee Medal (Ten Years of the Independence of Kazakhstan)

2002 – Kazakhstan Respublikasynyn Karuli Kushterine 10 Zhyl Jubilee Medal (Ten Years of the Armed Forces of the Republic of Kazakhstan)

2005 – Tynga 50 Zhyl Jubilee Medal (Fifty Years of the Virgin)

2004 – Kazakhstan Temir Zholy 100 Zhyl Jubilee Medal (One-hundred Years of Kazakh Rail Transport)

2005 – 1941–45 Uly Otan Sogysyndagy Zheniske 60 Zhyl Jubilee Medal (Sixty Years Since Victory in the Great Patriotic War 1941–45)

2005 – Kazakhstan Konstitutsiasina 10 Zhyl Jubilee Medal (Ten Years of the Constitution of the Republic of Kazakhstan)

2005 – Kazakhstan Republicaskynyn Parlamentine 10 Zhyl Jubilee Medal (Ten Years of Parliament in the Republic of Kazakhstan)

2008 – Astananyn 10 Zhyly Jubilee Medal (Ten Years of Astana)

2011 – Kazakhstan Respublikanskynyn Tauelsizdigine 20 Zhyl Jubilee Medal (Twenty Years of Independence of the Republic of Kazakhstan)

Other Honours

1996 – Badge of the President of the Republic of Kazakhstan

2011 – Badge of Elbasy Special Sample (Senate of the Parliament of the Republic of Kazakhstan)

Honours of Social Organizations of the Republic of Kazakhstan

Medals

1997 – Gold Medal of the Union of Architects of the Republic of Kazakhstan

1999 – Honorary Order of Peace and Accord (Hebrew Congress of Kazakhstan)

2002 – Gold Medal Laureate of the International Award named after Khoja Ahmed Yasawi (International Kazakh-Turkish University named after Khoja Ahmed Yasawi)

2003 – Gold Medal of the Eurasian National University named after L.N. Gumilev

2006 – Large Gold Medal for Major Contribution to Science (National Academy of Science of the Republic of Kazakhstan)

2007 – World Ambassador Medal (Children of the World International Cultural Centre)

2009 – Gold Medal of the Union of Town Builders of Kazakhstan

2009 – Gold Medal of the Kazakh National University named after al-Farabi

2011 – Birlik Gold Medal (National Assembly of Kazakhstan)

Awards

1997 – International Award of National Accord

2003 – Award named after L.N. Gumilev (Eurasian National University named after L.N. Gumilev)

Other Honours

1999 – Gold Sign of Ana Tildin Aibary (Kazakh Tili International Community)

2000 – Rank of Man of the Century (Social Council of the Abylai Khan International Trust, the Kazakh Society of Security of Historical and Cultural Monuments, and the Altyn Adam Trust)

2008 – Baurzhan Momyshuly Commemorative Honorary Sign for Ninety Years (the Kazakh Association of Veterans of the Kazakh War)

2011 – Rank of Gasyr Gulamasy (National Science Academy of the Republic of Kazakhstan)

State Honours from Foreign Countries

Orders

1995 – Commemorative Gold Order of Manas-10,000 (Kyrgyz Republic)

1997 – Order of Prince Yaroslav the Wise First Degree (Ukraine)

1997 – Great Cross Large Ribbon for Service before the Italian Republic (Italy)

1998 – Order of the Sacred Apostle Andrew (Russian Federation)

1998 – Order of Buyuk Hizmatlari Uchin, for Outstanding Achievements (Republic of Uzbekistan)

1999 – Large Cross of the Order of the Star of Romania (Romania)

2000 – Large Star of Merit of the Austrian Republic (Austria)

2000 – Order of Vytautus the Great of Lithuania (Lithuania)

2000 – Order of Ismoli Somoni (Republic of Tajikistan)

2000 – Large Cross of the Order of Saint Michael and Saint George (Great Britain and Republic of Ireland)

2001 – Large Cross of the Order of Saviours (Greece)

2001 – Order of King Tomoslav Large Ribbon with the Sign of the Great Damica (Croatia)

2001 – Order of Pia (Vatican State)

2002 – Gold Order of Freedom (Slovenia)

2002 – Order of the White Eagle (Poland)

2004 – Order of the Grand Necklace of Badr (Kingdom of Saudi Arabia)

2006 – Large Ribbon of the Order of Leopold I (Belgium)

2007 – Order of 'Independence' (Qatar)

2007 – Order of the White Double Cross First Degree (Slovakia)

2007 – Large Cross of the Order of Merit (Hungary)

2007 – Order of the Great Nile (Egypt)

2008 – Large Cross of the Order of the Honorary Legion (France)

2008 – Order of Chrysanthemum Grand Cordon (Japan)

2008 – Large Cross of the Order of the Oak Crown (Luxembourg)

2008 – Order of Erdene Ochir (Mongolia)

2008 – Order of Zayed (United Arab Emirates)

2009 – Order of Mugunghwa (the Eternally Blossoming Rose) (Republic of Korea)

2009 – Order of the Turkish Republic First Class (Turkey)

2010 – Order of Liberty (Ukraine)

2011 – Order of the Cross of Mary Land (Estonia)

Medals

1994 – Commemorative medals of the Senate and Congress of Deputies of General Cortes of Spain (Spain)

1995 – Commemorative Gold Medal in Commemoration of the 1000-Year Epic Manas (Kyrgyz Republic)

1997 – Medal in Memory of 850 Years of Moscow (Russian Federation)

2003 – Medal in Memory of 300 Years of Saint Petersburg (Russian Federation)

2003 – 200 years of Establishment of the Bukeyev Horde Jubilee Medal (Russian Federation)

2003 – Medal for Achievement (Finland)

2005 – Commemorative Medal in Honour of Agreement on the State Borders between the Russian Federation and the Republic of Kazakhstan (Russian Federation)

2007 – Jubilee Medal of 140 Years of the Romanian Parliament (Romania)

Other Honours

1999 – Order for Service (Republic of Ingushetia of the Russian Federation)

2007 – Order of Akhmad Kadyrov (Chechen Republic of the Russian Federation)

Honours from International Organizations

Orders

1997 – Golden Olympic Order (International Olympics Committee)

2000 – Silver Order of the International Association of Amateur Boxing for Outstanding Service

2002 – Gold Order of the International Association of Amateur Boxing for Outstanding Service

2003 – Gold Order of the International Association of Boxing

2007 – Gold Order of the Olympic Committee of Asia

Medals

1993 – Gold Medal and Honorary Diploma of Man of the Year (Rukhaniyat International Association for the Revival of Spirituality, Kyrgyz Republic)

1999 – Medal of the International Academy of Technological Sciences (Russian Federation)

1999 – Large Silver Medal of the International Academy of Engineers (Russian Federation)

1999 – Medal of the International Trust for the Health of the Family (Turkey)

1999 – Gold Medal for Services to Information Technology (International Academy of Information, Russian Federation)

2000 – Medal of the International Academy of Arts (Russian Federation)

2000 – Large Gold Medal of the International Academy of Engineers (Russian Federation)

2002 – Gold Medal of the Tree of Friendship (Union of the Inter-parliamentary assembly and interstate TV/Radio Company Mir)

2003 – Gold Medal for Investment in the Development of CIS (International Council of the Organizing Committee of the International Olympus Competition)

2003 – Gold Medal of Plato for Service in the Development of Education (International Academy of Information, Russian Federation)

2005 – Medal for Ten Years of the Association of Universities of Caspian States

Awards

1996 – Award of the International Crane-Montana Forum (Swiss Confederation)

1999 – Golden Atlantis Award (International Academy of Technological Sciences, Russian Federation)

1999 – Award of Dove of Peace (UNESCO Dodecanese Islands, Greece)

2003 – International Award of the International Union of the Organizational Committee of the International Olympus Competition

2004 – International Award named after Maimonides (International Awards Committee named after Maimonides, Israel)

2010 – Themis High Judicial Award (International Lawyers Union, Russian Federation)

2011 – Award of the World Public Forum, Dialogue of Civilizations (Greece)

Other Honours

1996 – Special Prize for Investment in the Business Development of the International Crane-Montana Forum 96 (Swiss Confederation)

1999 – Banner of Peace of International Agreement for the Security of Artistic and Scientific Institutions and Historical Monuments (Roerich Pact)

1999 – Diploma for Outstanding Contribution to the Advancement of Democracy (International Election System Trust, USA)

2001 – Diploma of Outstanding Engineer of the Twentieth Century (International Academy of Engineers, Russian Federation)

2002 – Sign of Honour of the International Union of Architects (France)

2003 – Honorary Sign of International Confederations of Sports Organizations

2007 – Jubilee Sign of Fifteen Years of the Agreement of Collective Security

2010 – Honorary Gold Sign for Service before the Trade Union Movement (General Confederation of Trade Unions, Russian Federation)

Honours of the Social Organizations of Foreign Countries

Orders

1996 – Order of Holy Prince Daniel of Moscow First Degree (Russian Orthodox Church, Russian Federation)

2005 – Order for Contribution to the Development of Society (Russian Academy of Natural Sciences, Russian Federation)

2005 – Order for Services to Science in Metallurgy (Moscow Institute of Steel and Alloy, Russian Federation)

2005 – Order of Holy Pious Prince Dmitri Donskoy First Degree (Russian Orthodox Church, Russian Federation)

2006 – Al-Fakhr Order First Degree (Muftis of the Russia Union, Russian Federation)

2010 – Order of Glory and Honour (Russian Orthodox Church, Russian Federation)

Medals

1993 – Large Gold Medal of the Guild of Economic Development and Marketing of the City of Nuremburg (Germany)

1994 – Emmori Medal (Georgetown University, USA)

1997 – Medal for Spiritual Unity (Muftis of the Russia Union, Russian Federation)

1998 – Medal for International Understanding (Unity International Trust, India)

2000 – Star of the Blue Planet Medal (Russian Space-aviation Agency, Russian Federation)

2001 – Gold Medal of the City of Athens (Greece)

2002 – Commemorative Medal of the International Programme of the Initiative for the Prevention of Nuclear War (USA)

2009 – High Honour of the National Olympic Committee of the Chinese National Republic (KNR)

Awards

1991 – Award named after Gregory Skovoroda (Kiev Innovation and Political Centre, Ukraine SSR)

1992 – International Literary Prize of Capri (Italy)

1998 – Award for Contribution to the Development of the Relationship between Nations of the Turkic World (Writers and Artists of the Turkic World Trust, Turkey)

1999 – Award for Services to the Turkic World (Writers and Artists of the Turkic World Trust, Turkey)

2006 – Award for Service to the Turkish World (Writers and Artists of the Turkic World Trust, Turkey)

2007 – International Award of Peace (Nova South-Eastern University, USA)

2010 – Award of Peace and Preventative Diplomacy (East-west Institute, USA)

2011 – Award for Brave Leadership of a Pioneer, which gave an Example for Reducing the Nuclear Threat (the Nuclear Threat Initiative, USA)

Other Honours

1998 – Honour of the 'Torch of Liberty' (Volunteers of America, USA)

2000 – Sign of Honour, Diploma Certificate (Israel)

2000 – Sign of Distinction of the Honorary Citizen of the City of Dneprodzerzhinsk (Ukraine)

2002 – Gold Sign of Miner of Russia (High Mining Union of Mining Operators of Russia and the Cooperative Development of Mining Industry and Sciences Trust, Russian Federation).

2003 – Cross of Honour for the Revival of Ukraine First Degree (Ukrainian Trust for Science-Economic and Legal Cooperation, Ukraine)

2004 – Jubilee Breastplate of 250 Years of MSU named after M.V. Lomonosov (Russian Federation)

2007 – Honorary Award of the Gold Biatek (Economic Club, Slovakia)

2007 – Commemorative Sign, Best System of Management amongst Muslim States (Pakistan Observer English language edition, Pakistan)

Honorary Citizenship

1991 – Honorary citizen of Duluth (USA)

1991 – Honorary citizen of Temirtau (Kazakh SSR)

1994 – Honorary citizen of Madrid (Spain)

1995 – Honorary citizen of Almaty (Kazakhstan)

1996 – Honorary citizen of Tbilisi (Greece)

1998 – Honorary citizen of Bucharest (Romania)

1998 – Honorary citizen of Astana (Kazakhstan)

1999 – Honorary citizen of Sofia (Bulgaria)

2000 – Honorary citizen of Bayan-Ulgii Aimak (Mongolia)

2000 – Honorary citizen of Dneprodzerzhinsk (Ukraine)

2001 – Honorary citizen of Athens (Greece)

2002 – Honorary citizen of Ridder (Kazakhstan)

2002 – Honorary citizen of Karaganda (Kazakhstan)

2003 – Honorary citizen of Seoul (Republic of Korea)

2008 – Honorary citizen of the Mangistau region (Kazakhstan)

2009 – Honorary citizen of the Hainan province (China)

2009 – Honorary citizen of Calgary (Canada)

Bibliography

WORKS BY N.A. NAZARBAYEV

Books

- *Steel Profile of Kazakhstan*, Alma-Ata: Kazakhstan, 1985
- *Without Right and Left*, M.: The Young Guard, 1991
- *Strategy of Resource and Market Transition*, M.: Mechanical Engineering, 1992
- *A Strategy of Formation and Development of Kazakhstan as a Sovereign State*, Almaty: Deuir, 1992
- *Ideological Consolidations of Society as a Condition for Progress in Kazakhstan*, Almaty: FPI Twenty-first Century Kazakhstan, 1993
- *For the Renewal of Kazakhstan through Clear Reforms*, Almaty: Kazakhstan, 1994
- *Market and Socio-Economic Development*, M.: Economics, 1994
- *On the Threshold of the Twenty-first Century*, Almaty: Oner, 1996
- *Five Years of Independence: From Reports, Speeches and Articles of the President of the Republic of Kazakhstan*, Almaty: Kazakhstan, 1996
- *Eurasian Union: Idea, Practice, Perspective (1994–1997)*, M.: Trust for the Assistance of Developing Social and Political Sciences, 1997
- *Lessons from History and Modernity*, Almaty: Kazakhstan, 1997
- *Kazakh-Russian Relations*, M.: Consumer Price Index 'Russian Rarity', 1997
- *In the Stream of History*, Almaty: Atamura, 1999
- *Strategic Transformation of Society and the Renewal of Eurasian Civilization*, M.: Economics, 2000

• *Epicentre of Peace*, Astana: Elorda, 2001

• *A Critical Decade*, Almaty: Atamura, 2003

• *Strategy of Independence*, Almaty: Atamura, 2005

• *In the Heart of Eurasia*, Almaty: Atamura, 2005

• *The Kazakhstan Way*, Karaganda, 2006; London 2008

• *Share Ideas with People*, Almaty: Mektep, 2007

• *The Strategy of Radical Renewal of Post-Industrial Society and Partnership Among Civilizations*, M.: Economics, 2008

• *Strategy for the Radical Renewal of the Global Community and Partnership of Civilizations*, Astana: LLP APKO, 2009

• *Selected Speeches of N.A. Nazarbayev: 1989–2009*, in Seven Volumes, Astana: Saryarka, 2010

• *Global Energy Strategy for Sustainable Development in the Twenty-first Century*, M.: Economics, 2011

Feature Articles

• 'Hello, "Green Mountain!"', *Lenin Change*, 7 August 1970

• 'Collective Efforts for Great Work Discipline', *Temirtauskiy Worker*, 27 February 1975

• 'Ranked as a laggard', *Pravda*, 29 December 1976

• 'Stages of Growth', *Economic Newspaper*, 18 August 1980

• 'Wealth from Waste', *Pravda*, 10 September 1982

• 'Milestones of the Coal Industry of Kazakhstan', *Coal*, No. 12, 1982

• 'The Most Important Condition of Intensification', *Pravda*, 22 May 1983

• 'The Master of Thrift', *Socialist Industry*, 10 September 1983

• 'The Effect of Unions: Experiences and Challenges', *Economic Newspaper*, 28 September 1983

• 'New Conditions "Brake" the Old', *Pravda*, No.17, 1987

• 'The Economy of Kazakhstan: the Reality and Prospects for Renewal', *Pravda*, 18 February 1989

• 'Only the Start of the Transition', *Labour,* 5 June 1988

- 'Problems with the Division of Labour', *Pravda*, 1 February 1989
- 'Problems with the Aral Sea and Means of Resolving Them', *Pravda*, 18 February 1989
- 'We Have to Build a Direct Interaction', *Pravda*, 18 February 1989
- 'Freed from Stagnation', *Party Life*, No. 11, 1990
- 'In the Name of Renewal', *Economics and Life*, No. 30, 1990
- 'Together in the Renewal of the Union We Will Beat All Hardships', *Red Star,* 16 March 1991
- 'Consistently and Persistently Introduce Market Relations', *Pravda*, 5 July 1991
- 'Inviolable Boundaries', *Komsomolskaya Pravda*, 22 November 1991
- 'Time is Money', *Komsomolskaya Pravda*, 22 November 1991
- 'Strengthening Independence Through Stable Development', *Pravda*, 16 December 1991
- 'Terra Incognita Post-totalitarian Democracy', *Europe and the World*, No. 2, 1992
- 'From the Imperial USSR to the Community of an Independent State', *Pravda*, 10 March 1992
- 'The Republic does not need Credit but Investment', *Business People*, No. 10, 1992
- 'Chaos and Anarchy do not Fit the Market', *Russian Newspaper,* 20 November 1992
- 'Between the Past and the Future', *Labour*, 31 December 1992
- 'Unite – We Will Live!', *Work Tribune*, 6 February 1993
- 'The Ghost of Public Poverty Wanders through the CIS', *Moscow News*, 11 April 1993
- 'Our Landmarks – Consolidation, Communal Progress', *Social Partnership*, Council of Kazakhstan, 13 May 1993
- 'International Unity and Economic Sovereignty – the Reliable Support of our Progress', *Council of Kazakhstan*, 14 October 1993
- 'Word About Abay', *Pravda*, 1 January 1994
- 'The Union without the Hammer and Sickle', *Moscow News,* 17–24 April 1994

- 'On Speeding up the Market Conversion and Measures for Leaving the Economic Crisis', *Kazakhstan Herald*, 11 June 1994

- 'Not the USSR, and not the CIS', *Independent Newspaper*, 8 July 1994

- 'Eurasian Space: Integration Potential and its Implementation', *Panorama*, 24 September 1994

- 'A View of the World Order, Development and Democratization', *Kazakhstan and the World Community*, No. 1, 1994

- 'Our Hard but Fair Path', *Economic News Russia and the Commonwealth*

- 'The New Constitution should be a National Agreement with Power and Serve as a Basis for the Unification of all Inhabitants of the Republic into One Kazakh Nation', *Panorama*, No. 27, 1995

- 'Towards Shared Goals at Different Speeds', *Independent Newspaper,* 29 March 1996

- 'I am First and Foremost a Supporter of Post-Soviet Space', *Realists' Club*, No. 21, 1996

- 'Socialist Syndrome', *Moscow News*, 22–29 June, 1997

- 'We will Build an Open Society', *Literary Russia*, 27 June 1997

- 'Lessons and Prospects', *Independent Newspaper,* 10 July 1997

- 'About the Commonwealth of Independent States', *Economic News Russia and the Commonwealth*, No. 21, 1997

- 'Kazakhstan will Inevitably Become a Flourishing Country', *Izvestiya*, 4 June 1998

- 'Store memory, Strengthen the Agreement', *Pravda*, 16 January 1998

- 'Wealth must be Distributed Intelligently', *Economic News*, No. 13, 1998

- 'December 1986: How it Was', *Evening Almaty*, 4 January 1999

- 'Constitution – the Basis for the Stability and Flourishing of Kazakhstan', *Pravda*, 30 August 2000

- 'Don't let Isolation Hijack Progression', *Economic News Russia and the Commonwealth*

- 'How will we Divide the Caspian Sea', *Izvestia-Kazakhstan*, 5 October 2002

• 'Forever Together: for the 250-year Voluntary Union of Kazakhstan and Russia', *Agitator*, No. 11, 1982

• 'The Effect of Unification: Experience and Problems', *Economic Newspaper,* 28 September 1983

• 'Speech at the Tenth Session of the Supreme Council of the Kazakh SSR Tenth Convocation', *Pravda*, 6 December 1984

• 'Speech at the Celebratory Ceremony for Sixty Years since the Formation of Uzbek SSR and the Communist Party of Uzbekistan', *Pravda Vostoka*, 9 December 1984

• 'Speech at the Celebratory Ceremony for Sixty Years since the Formation of the Tajik SSR and the Communist Party of Tajikistan', *Communist Tajikistan*, 16 December 1984

• 'Speech at the Fourth Session of the Supreme Council of the USSR Eleventh Convocation', 26–27 November 1985, *Stenographer's Report*, M., 1985, C. 86-91

• 'Speech at the Fourth Session of the Supreme Union of the USSR Eleventh Convocation 26–27 November 1985', *Izvestia*, 28–29 November 1985

• 'Speech at the Twenty-seventh Congress of the CPSU, 25 February–6 March 1986', *Stenographer's Report*, M., 1986, C. 129–31

• 'Speech at the Fourth Session of the Supreme Council Eleventh Convocation "On the State Plan for Economic and Social development of the Kazakh SSR from 1986-1990"', *Pravda*, 5 July 1986

• 'Speech at the Seminar for Local Employees "Improvement of Territorial Management – the Crucial Management of the Reconstruction of the Economy"', *Pravda*, 5 July 1986

• 'Speech at the Eigth Session of the Supreme Soviet Council of the USSR Eleventh Convocation', *Pravda*, 22 October 1987

• 'Speech at the Eleventh Plenary Session of the Central Committee of the Communist Party of Kazakhstan "On the Challenges of the Republican Party of Organizing the Long-term Expansion of the Consumer Goods Industry, the Development of Payment Services, the Guarantee of a Balance of Incomes and Outgoings of the Population"', *Pravda*, 10 February 1988

• 'Speech at the Nineteenth All-union Conference "Cutting the Gross Knot"', *Pravda*, 10 July 1988

• 'Speech at the Celebratory Assembly for the Seventy-first Anniversary of the Great October Revolution "Past the October Revolution on the Path to Renewal"', *Pravda*, 7 November 1989.

• 'Speech at the Republican Meeting for Problems with the Aral Sea', *Lenin's Path*, 7 February 1989

• 'Speech "About the economy"', *Pravda*, 1 June 1989

• 'Publication at the Seventh Session of the Supreme Council of the USSR Tenth Convocation', *Pravda*, 25 November 1982

• 'Forever Together: for the 250-year Voluntary Union of Kazakhstan and Russia', *Agitator*, No. 11, 1982

• 'The Effect of Unification: Experience and Problems', *Economic Newspaper*, 28 September 1983

• 'Speech at the Tenth Session of the Supreme Council of the Kazakh SSR Tenth Convocation', *Pravda*, 6 December 1984

• 'Speech at the Celebratory Ceremony for Sixty Years since the Formation of Uzbek SSR and the Communist Party of Uzbekistan', *Pravda Vostoka*, 9 December 1984

• 'Speech at the Celebratory Ceremony for Sixty Years since the Formation of the Tajik SSR and the Communist Party of Tajikistan', *Communist Tajikistan*, 16 December 1984

• 'Speech at the Fourth Session of the Supreme Council of the USSR Eleventh Convocation', 26–27 November 1985, *Stenographer's Report*, M., 1985, C. 86-91

• 'Speech at the Fourth Session of the Supreme Union of the USSR Eleventh Convocation 26–27 November 1985', *Izvestia*, 28–29 November 1985

• 'Speech at the Twenty-seventh Congress of the CPSU, 25 February–6 March 1986', *Stenographer's Report*, M., 1986, C. 129–31

• 'Speech at the Fourth Session of the Supreme Council Eleventh Convocation "On the State Plan for Economic and Social development of the Kazakh SSR from 1986-1990"', *Pravda*, 5 July 1986

• 'Speech at the Seminar for Local Employees "Improvement of Territorial Management – the Crucial Management of the Reconstruction of the Economy"', *Pravda*, 5 July 1986

• 'Speech at the Eigth Session of the Supreme Soviet Council of the USSR Eleventh Convocation', *Pravda*, 22 October 1987

• 'Speech at the Eleventh Plenary Session of the Central Committee of the Communist Party of Kazakhstan "On the Challenges of the Republican Party of Organizing the Long-term Expansion of the Consumer Goods Industry, the Development of Payment Services, the Guarantee of a Balance of Incomes and

Outgoings of the Population"', *Pravda*, 10 February 1988

• 'Speech at the Nineteenth All-union Conference "Cutting the Gross Knot"', *Pravda*, 10 July 1988

• 'Speech at the Celebratory Assembly for the Seventy-first Anniversary of the Great October Revolution "Past the October Revolution on the Path to Renewal"', *Pravda*, 7 November 1989.

• 'Speech at the Republican Meeting for Problems with the Aral Sea', *Lenin's Path*, 7 February 1989

• 'Speech "About the economy"', *Pravda*, 1 June 1989

BOOKS ABOUT N.A. NAZARBAYEV

Published in the Russian Language

• Valovoy, D. Кремлевский тупик и Назарбаев (The Kremlin Deadlock and Nazarbayev). Young Guard, 1993.

• Bekturganov, N. Изучение трудов Президента Республики Казахстан Н.А. Назарбаев, посвященных коренным вопросам преобразования общества. (A Study of the Works by President of the Republic of Kazakhstan N.A. Nazarbayev, Dedicated to Fundamental Issues Transforming the Society). Karaganda, 1994.

• Buluktayev, Y.U. Выборы Президента Республики Казахстана: Опыт сравнительного политико-правого анализа (The Elections of the President of the Republic of Kazakhstan: an Attempt at a Comparative Politico-legal Analysis). Almaty: Institute for the Development of Kazakhstan, 1994.

• Dzhunusova, Z.H. Республика Казахстан: Президент, Институты демократии (On the Republic of Kazakhstan: The President, Democratic Institutions). Almaty: Zheti Zhargi, 1996.

• Simashko, M. Дорога на святую землю (Road to the Sacred Land). Almaty: Zhibek Zholi, 1996.

• Bazaryaninov, V., Tsiganok, N. Предсказание – историко публицистический очерк (Foresight – an Historico-publicistic Essay). Dnipropetrovsk: Porogi (Thresholds), 1997.

• Tokayev, K.K. Под стягом независимости. Очерки о внешней политике Казахстана (Under the Banner of Independence: Essays on the Foreign Policy of Kazakhstan). Almaty: Bilim, 1997.

• Vidova, O.I. Нурсултан Назарбаев: Портрет человека и политика (Nursultan Nazarbayev: A Personal and Political Portrait). Almaty: Bilim, 1997.

• Maylybayev, B.A. Институт Президента: традиции демократического конституционализма и опыт Республики Казахстана (Presidential Institution: Traditions of a Democratic Constitutionalism and the Experience of the Republic of Kazakhstan). Almaty: Complex, 1998.

• Kasymbekov, M.B. Становление института президентсва в Республике Казахстан. (The Foundation of the Institution of President in the Republic of Kazakhstan). Astana: Elorda, 2000.

• Kim, V. Годы созидания : Анализ политических и конституционно-правовых взглядов Первого Президента Республики Казахстан (The Years of Creating: an Analysis of Political and Legal-Consititional Views of the First President of the Republic of Kazakhstan). Almaty: Edelweiss, 2000.

• Nysanbayev, A.N. (editor) Мир о Назарбаеве (The World Around Nazarbayev). Almaty: Kazakh Encyclopedia, 2000.

• Президент Нурсултан Назарбаев. Стратегия вечной дружбы. Казахстан–Россия (President Nursultan Nazarbayev. Strategy for Eternal Friendship: Kazakhstan–Russia). LLC Russkiy Raritet, 2000.

• Retivikh, A.V. Казахстан на стыке веков. Историческая роль Президента Республики Казахстан Н.А. Назарбаев в формировании геополитической стратегии государства (Kazakhstan at the Juncture of Two Centuries: the Historical Role of the President of the Republic of Kazakhstan, N.A. Nazarbayev, in the Formation of the State's Geopolitical Strategy). Almaty: Gylym, 2000.

• Spayev, T. Он в будущем (The Man in the Future). Shymkent: Zhibek Zholy, 2000.

• Tolmachev, G.I. Лидер. Документальная повесть о первом Президенте Республики Казахстан Н.А. Назарбаеве (Leader: a Documentary Account of the First President of the Republic of Kazakhstan N.A. Nazarbayev). Almaty: Deuir, 2000.

• Ertysbayev, E.K. Казахстан и Назарбаев: Логика перемен (Kazakhstan and Nazarbayev: the Logic of Change). Astana: Elorda, 2001.

• Maylybayev, B.A. Становление и эволюция института Президента Республики Казахстан: проблемы, тенденции, перспективы: опыт полтитко-правового исследования: монография (The Foundation and Evolution of the Institution of the President of the Republic of Kazakhstan: Problems, Tendencies, Prospects – an Attempt at a Political-legal Study). Almaty: Arys, 2001.

• Tuimebayev, Z.K., Baybek, B.K. (editors) Серия 'Один год Президента', 2001–7 годы (Series 'One Year of the President', 2001–7), in seven tomes. Astana, 2001–7.

• Kasymbekov, M.B. Институт президенства как инструмент политической модернизации (The Institution of the Presidency as an Instrument of Political Modernization). Astana, 2002.

• Allaniyazov, T.K. История Казахстана в трудах Н.А. Назарбаев: Учебное пособие (A History of Kazakhstan in the Works of N.A. Nazarbayev: a Textbook). Almaty: Twenty-first Century Foundation, 2003.

• Bazaryaninov, V., Yezhevskiy, L., Zhandauletov, V. Своими Глазами: историко-публицистический очерк (Through His Eyes: a Historico-publicistic Essay). Dneprodzerzhinsk, 2003.

• Vidova, O.I. Нурсултан Назарбаев: Портрет человека и политика/2-е издание, дополненное. (Nursultan Nazarbayev: a Personal and Political Portrait/Second Edition, updated).

• Zholdasbekov, M.Z. Казахстан в XXI веке: Проблемы Евразийства и образования (Kazakhstan in the Twenty-first Century: Issues of Eurasia and its Formation). Astana: ENU Izvestia (News), 2003.

• Kasymbekov, M.B. Институт президенства: теория и практика/Уч. пособие (The Institution of the President: Theory and Practice/Textbook). Astana: Academy for State Services under the President of Kazakhstan, 2003.

• Tokayev, K.K. Преодоление: Дипломатические очерки (Meeting the Challenge: Diplomatic Essays). Almaty, 2003.

• Baikal, M., Ibrahimov, A.I. Настройщик Евразии (The Builder of Eurasia). M.: Eurasia, 2004.

• Dymov, O.H. Мы, народ Казахстана (We, the Nation of Kazakhstan). Astana, 2004.

• Dugin, A.H. Евразийская миссия Нурсултана Назарбаева (Nursultan Nazarbayev's Eurasian Mission). M.: Euraia, 2004.

• Mailybayev, B.A. Послания Президента в потоке истории (политический анализ, документы, публицистика) (The President's Message in the Stream of History [Political Analysis, Documents, Political Essays]). Almaty: Complex, 2004.

• Азиатский прорыв (The Asian Breakthrough). Astana: Free Society, 2005.

• Dudki, E. (editor) Казахстан: история успеха глазами мирового сообщества (Kazakhstan: Success Story through the Eyes of Global Society). Almaty: Taimas Publishing House, 2005.

• Under the general editorship of Aliev, Zh.A. Назарбаев Н.А. - основатель казахстанской модели межэтнического и межконфессионального согласия (N.A. Nazarbayev – Founder of the Kazakh Model for Interethnic and Interreligious Accord). Almaty: Zheti Zhargy, 2005.

• Saadanbekov, Z. Нурсултан Назарбаев: Законы Лидерства. (Nursultan Nazarbayev: Rules of Leadership). Astana: Kultegin, 2005.

• Sadykov T.T. Интеллектуальный облик будущего. (Intellectual Outlook of the Future). Almaty: Edelweiss, 2005.

• XXI век: Политики, духовные лидеры, интеллектуалы и биснесмены мира о Н.А. Назарбаеве (Politicians, Spiritual Leaders, Intellectuals and Businessmen of the World on N.A. Nazarbayev). Almaty: Atamura, 2005.

• Kvyatovski, O. Время наших побед (The Time of Our Victory). Astana: Edelweiss, 2007.

• Kasymbekov, M.B., Moldagarinov, A.M., Alibekov, A.C., (editors) Награда Президенту – признательность народу (An Award to the President is Acknowledgement for the Nation). Almaty: Oner, 2007.

• Galasieva, A.M. (editor) Основы имиджелогии на примере Первого Президентства, 2-е изд. (Foundations of Image Studies on the Example of the First Presidency, second edition). Ust-Kamenogorsk: VKGU Publishing House, 2007.

• Solozobova, Y.M. Путь к лидерству: социально-экономические и политические реформы в Казахстане

(The Path to Leadership: Socio-Economic and Political Reforms in Kazakhstan). M. Boslen, 2007.

• Tokayev, K.K. Свет и тень (Light and Shade). Astana, 2007.

• Sagynali, A.C., Kaipovoi, B.M. Инициативы главы государства в становлении и формировании модели стратегического управления. Сборник выступлений и статей (Initiatives of the Head of State in the Formation and Foundation of Models of Strategic Management). Almaty: Taimas Publishing House, 2008.

• Kasymbekov, M.B. Первый. Очерки о Президенте Республики Казахстан (The First. Essays on the President of the Republic of Kazakhstan). Astana: Foliant, 2008.

• Makhashev, N.M. Казахстан: эпохи Нурсултана Назарбаева (Kazakhstan: Epoch of Nursultan Nazarbayev). Almaty: Olke, 2008.

• Medvedev, R. Нурсултан Назарбаев: Казахстанский прорыв и Евразийский проект (Nursultan Nazarbayev: the Kazakh Breakthrough and the Eurasian Project). M. BBPG, 2008.

• Shaikhtdunov, M.E. (editor) Современный Казахстан: стратегия успеха (Modern Kazakhstan: Strategy for Success). Almaty: Taimas Publishing House, 2008.

• Инициатива Президента Республики Казахстан о региальной интеграции в рамках Союза центральноазиатских государств (СЦАГ)/Материалы круглого стола, г. Алматы, 18 ноября 2009 года (Initiatives of the President of the Republic of Kazakhstan in the Framework of the Union of Central Asian States [UCSA]/Materials from the Round Table). Almaty, 18 November 2009.

• Назарбаев Нурсултан Абишевич: основатель независимого государства (Nazarbayev Nursultan Abishevich: Founder of an Independent State). Astana, 2009.

• Aitken, J. Нурсултан Назарбаев и созидание Казахстана (Nazarbayev and the Making of Kazakhstan). M. Artistic Literature, 2010.

• At-Turki, Majed ben Adbel Aziz. Свет власти в Казахстане: Президент Нурсултан Назарбаев (The Light of Power in Kazakhstan: President Nursultan Nazarbayev). Arabian Printing & Publishing House, 2010.

• Mukhamejanov, V.H., Sagyngali, A.S., Aktayeva, K.K. В знак уважения и признательность... (дипломатические подарки, преподнесенные Президенту Республики Казахстан Н.А. Назарбаеву): Альбом (As a Sign of Respect and Recognition... [Diplomatic Gifts brought to the President of the Republic of Kazakhstan N.A. Nazarbayev] Album). Astana: MPP RK, 2010.

• Sarybai, K.S. Внешнеполитическая деятельность Президента Республики Казахстан Н.А. Назарбаев в 2009 году (Foreign Political Activity of the President of the Republic of Kazakhstan, N.A. Nazarbayev, in 2009). Almaty: KISI, 2010.

• Guzman, M.S. Формула Власти: 60 интервью в золотом галстуке (Formula of Power: Sixty Interviews in the Golden Tie). M.: Terra, 2010.

• Nysanbayev, A.N., Dunayev, V.Y. (editors) Евразийская доктрина Нурсултана Назарбаева (The Eurasian Doctrine of Nursultan Nazarbayev). Almaty: 2010.

• Esimbai, S. Ушконыр: моя золотая колыбель (Ushkonyr: My Golden Cradle). Almaty: Kitap, 2010.

• Sagyngali, A.S., Kaipovoi, B.M. Интеграционные инициативы Первого Президента Республики Казахстан Н.А. Назарбаев (Initiatives for Integration of the First President of the Republic of Kazakhstan, N.A. Nazarbayev). Astana: MPP RK, 2010.

• Kaletayev, D.A. Модернизация на постсоветском пространстве: фактор национального лидера (Modernization in a Post-Soviet Space: the Factor of the National Leader). Astana: Institute of Contemporary Politics, 2010.

• Kasymbekov, M.B. Лидер и Независимость (Leader and Independence). Almaty: Kazakh Encyclopaedia, 2010.

• Лидер глобального антиядерного движения: Лидер нации (Leader of the Global Anti-nuclear Movement: Leader of the Nation). Astana: Business World of Astana, 2010.

• Млечин Л.М. Назарбаев: Групповой портрет с президентом (Nazarbayev: a Group Portrait with the President). M.: Vostok-Zapad (East-West), 2010.

• Назарбаев Нурсултан Абишевич – основатель независимого государства (Nazarbayev Nursultan Abishevich – Founder of the Independent State). Almaty: Kazakh Encyclopaedia, 2010.

• Musin, N.K. (editor) Н.А. Назарбаев и Астана (N.A. Nazarbayev and Astana). Astana: Business World of Astana, 2010.

• Nysanbayev, A.N., Kosichenko, A.H. Н.А. Назарбаев: основоположник казахстанской модели межэтнического и межконфессиального согласия (N.A. Nazarbayev: a Founder of the Kazakh Model of Interethnic and Interfaith Accord). Almaty: Institute of Philosophy and Political Studies, 2010.

• Нурсултан Назарбаев на исторической ленте РИА Новости (Nursultan Nazarbayev in the historic newsfeed of RIA News). Astana: Business World of Astana, 2010.

• Sagyngali, A.S., Kaipovoi, B.M. Первый Президент Республики Казахстан и формирование правового государства (The First President of the Republic of Kazakhstan and the Formation of a Legal State). Almaty: Taimas Publishing House, 2010.

• Председательство Республики Казахстан в ОБСЕ: Доверие, традиции, транспарентность, толерантность. Путь в Европу. Казахстан – Председатель ОБСЕ (Chairmanship of the Republic of Kazakhstan in the OSCE: Trust, Traditions, Transparency and Tolerance. The Path to Europe. Kazakhstan – the OSCE Chair). Astana: Business World of Astana, 2010.

• Sultanov (editor) Президент Н.А. Назарбаев и современный Казахстан: Сборник документов и материалов в 3-х томах (President N.A. Nazarbayev and Modern Kazakhstan: a Collection of Documents and Materials in Three Tomes). Almaty: KISI, 2010.

• Solozobova (editor) Президентская власть в Казахстане: 20 лет успеха (Presidental Power in Kazakhstan: Twenty Years of Success). M.: Bilnet, 2010.

• Sarsenbai, K. Президент. Независимость (President. Independence). Almaty, 2010.

• Kasymbekov, M.B., Temirbolat, B.B. Серия 'Президент Республики Казахстан Нурсултан Назарбаев: Хроника деятельности'. 1990–2010 годы. В 16-ти томах ('The President of the Republic of Kazakhstan, Nursultan Nazarbayev: a Chronicle of Deeds' Series. 1990–2010. In Sixteen Tomes). Astana: Business World of Astana, 2010.

• Стратегический план – 2020: Казахстанский путь к лидерству (Strategic Plan – 2020: the Kazakh Journey to Leadership). Astana. Business World of Astana, 2010.

• Sultanov, B.K. Внешнеполитическая стратегия Президента Н.А. Назарбаева (Foreign Policy Strategy of President N.A. Nazarbayev). Astana: Foliant, 2010.

• Tokayev, K.K. Он делает историю (He Makes History). Astana: Foliant, 2010.

• Khan, G.B., Abdykarimov, O.A., Khan, I.G. Нурсултан Назарбаев: гуманизм и политическая воля. Историко-философский, политический анализ (Nursultan Nazarbayev: Humanism and Political Will. Historico-Philosophical and Political Analysis). Almaty: Raritet (Rarity), 2010.

• XXI век станет звездным веком Казахстана (The Twenty-first Century will be the Century of Triumph in Kazakhstan's History). Astana: Business World of Astana, 2010.

• Aitken, J. Казахстан: Сюрпризы и стереотипы (Kazakhstan: Surprises and Stereotypes after Twenty Years of Independence). M.: Artistic Literature, 2011.

• Karagizova, H.B., Makubayeva, D.S. Архитектор казахстанского успеха (Architect of Kazakh Success). Astana: MPP RK, 2011.

• Sultanov, B.K. (editor) Внешнеполитическая деятельность Президента Республики Казахстан Н.А. Назарбаева в 2010 году (Foreign Policy Activity of the President of the Republic of Kazakhstan N.A. Nazarbayev in 2010). Almaty: KISI, 2011.

• Sagynali, A.S., Kaipovoi, B.M. (editors) Внешнеполитические инициативы Н.А. Назарбаева: траектория сотрудничества Республики Казахстан и ОБСЕ (Foreign Policy Initiatives of N.A. Nazarbayev: Trajectory of Cooperation in the Republic of Kazakhstan and the OSCE). Almaty: MPP RK, 2011.

• Sagynali, A.S., Kaipovoi, B.M. (editors) Лидер Нации и Культуры: Сборник материалов и документов (Leader of the Nation and of Culture: a Collection of Materials and Documents). Astana: MPP RK, 2011.

• Sagynali, A.S., Kaipovoi, B.M. (editors) Лидер нации и независимость: Сборник научных статей и документов (Leader of the Nation and Independence: a Collection of

Research Papers and Documents). Astana: MPP RK, 2011.

• Mansurov, T.A. Евразийский проект Нурсултана Назарбаева, воплощенный в жизнь (Nursultan Nazarbayev's Eurasian Project that Turned into Reality). M.: Real Press, 2011.

• Zhumagulov, Professor B.T. Нурсултан Абишевич Назарбаев: Биобиблографический указатель в 5-ти томах (Nursultan Abishevich Nazarbayev: Bibliographical Guide in Five Tomes). Astana: Saryarka, 2011.

• Sagynali, A.S., Atayevoi, K.K. (editors) Президент и Независимость. Научно-фондовый сборник (The President and Independence. Scientific Files Collection). Astana: MPP RK, 2011.

• Kasymbekov, M.B., Moldagarinov, A.M. (editors) Размышления о лидере (Reflection on the Leader). Almaty: Kazakh Encyclopaedia, 2011.

• Saulebek A. Золотая колыбель Президента (The Golden Cradle of the President). Astana: Saryarka, 2011.